GW01081066

A Catechism and Confession of Faith

Robert Barclay

BIBLIOLIFE

A
CATECHISM
AND
CONFESSION OF FAITH,

APPROVED OF AND AGREED UNTO

BY THE

GENERAL ASSEMBLY

OF THE

PATRIARCHS, PROPHETS, AND APOSTLES, CHRIST HIMSELF CHIEF SPEAKER IN AND AMONG THEM.

Which containeth a true and faithful account of the principles and doctrines, which are most surely believed by the Churches of Christ in Great Britain and Ireland, who are reproachfully called by the name of Quakers; yet are found in the one Faith with the Primitive Church and Saints, as is most clearly demonstrated by some plain Scripture Testimonies, (without Consequences or Commentaries) which are here collected, and inserted by way of Answer to a few weighty, yet easy and familiar Questions, fitted as well for the wisest and largest, as for the weakest and lowest Capacities.—To which is added, an Expostulation with, and appeal to, all other Professors.

BY ROBERT BARCLAY.

Search the Scriptures, (or, ye search the Scriptures) for in them ye think ye have eternal Life, and they are they which testify of me. And ye will not come unto me, that ye might have Life.—John v. 39, 40.

PHILADELPHIA:
1843.

THE PREFACE

SINCE first that great apostacy took place in the hearts and heads of those who began, even in the apostles' days, to depart from the simplicity and purity of the gospel, as it was then delivered in its primitive splendour and integrity, innumerable have been the manifold inventions and traditions, the different and various notions and opinions, wherewith man, by giving way to the vain and airy imaginations of his own unstable mind, hath burthened the Christian faith. So that indeed, first by adding these things, and afterwards by equalling them, if not exalting them above the truth, they have at last come to be substituted in the stead of it; so that in process of time truth came to be shut out of doors, and another thing placed in the room thereof, having a show and a name, but wanting the substance and thing itself. Nevertheless, it pleased God to raise up witnesses for himself almost in every age and generation, who, according to the discoveries they received, bore some testimony, less or more, against the superstition and apostacy of the time; and in special manner, through the appearing of that light which first broke forth in Germany, about one hundred and fifty years ago, and afterwards reached divers other nations, the beast received a deadly wound; and a very great number did at one time protest against, and rescind from the church of Rome, in divers of their most gross and sensual doctrines and superstitious traditions. But, alas! it is for matter of lamentation, that the successors of these Protestants are establishing and building up in themselves that which their fathers were pulling down, instead of prosecuting and going on with so good and honourable a work, which will easily appear.

The generality of all Protestants, though in many other things miserably rent and shattered among themselves, do agree in dividing from the church of Rome in these two particulars.

First, That every principle and doctrine of the Christian faith is, and ought to be, founded upon the scriptures; and that whatsoever principles and doctrines are not only not contrary, but even not according thereto, ought to be denied as antichristian.

Secondly, That the scriptures themselves are plain and easy to be understood; and that every private Christian and member of the church ought to read and peruse them, that they may know their faith and belief founded upon them, and receive them for that cause alone, and not because any church or assembly has compounded and recommended them; the choicest and most pure of which, they are obliged to look upon as fallible.

Now, contrary to this their known and acknowledged principle, they do most vigorously prosecute and persecute others with the like severity the Papists did their fathers, for believing things that are plainly set down in the scriptures, and for not believing divers principles, for which themselves are forced to recur to tradition, and can by no means prove from scripture: to show which I shall not here insist, having allotted a chapter for it in the book itself; because to put it here, would swell it beyond the bounds of a preface.

Oh! how like do they show themselves, I mention it with regret, to the scribes and pharisees of old, who, of all men, most cried up and exalted Moses and the prophets, boasting greatly of being Abraham's children! And yet those were they that were the greatest opposers and vilifiers of Christ, to whom Moses and the prophets gave witness; yea, their chief accusations and exceptions against Christ were, as being a breaker of the law, and a blasphemer.

Can there any comparison run more parallel, seeing

there is now found a people, who are greatly persecuted, and bitterly reviled, and accused as heretics, by a generation that cry up and exalt the scriptures? And yet this people's principles are found in scripture, word by word; though the most grievous, and indeed the greatest calumny cast upon them is, that they vilify and deny the scriptures, and set up their own imaginations instead of them.

To disprove which, this Catechism and Confession of Faith is compiled, and presented to thy serious and impartial view. If thou lovest the scriptures indeed, and desirest to hold the plain doctrines there delivered, and not those strained and far-fetched consequences, which men have invented, thou shalt easily observe the whole principles of the people called Quakers, plainly couched in scripture words, without addition or commentary; especially in those things their adversaries oppose them in, where the scripture plainly decideth the controversy for them, without niceties and school-distinctions, which has been the wisdom by which the world hath not known God; and the words which have been multiplied without knowledge, by which counsel hath been darkened.

In the answers to the questions, there is not one word, that I know of, placed, but the express words of scripture; and if in some of the questions there be somewhat subsumed, of what in my judgment is the plain and naked import of the words, it is not to impose my sense upon the reader, but to make way for the next question, for the dependence of the matter's sake.

I shall leave it to the reason of any understanding and judicious man, who is not biassed by self-interest, that great enemy to true equity, and who in the least measure is willing to give way to the light of Christ in his conscience, if the scriptures do not pertinently and aptly answer to the questions?

As I have upon serious grounds separated from most of the confessions and catechisms heretofore published; so not without cause, I now have taken another method: they usually place their confession of faith before the catechism:

1 *

I judge it ought to be otherwise, in regard that which is easiest, and is composed for children, or such as are weak, ought in my judgment to be placed first; it being more regular to begin with things that are easy and familiar, and lead on to things that are more hard and intricate. Besides, that things be more largely opened in the catechism, and divers objections answered, which are proposed in the questions, the reader having passed through that first, will more perfectly understand the confession, which consisteth mainly in positive assertions.

Not long after I had received and believed the testimony I now bear, I had in my view both the possibility and facility of such a work; and now after a more large and perfect acquaintance with the holy scriptures, I found access to allow some time to set about it, and have also been helped to accomplish the same.

I doubt not but it might be enlarged by divers citations, which are here omitted as not being at present brought to my remembrance; yet I find cause to be contented, in that God hath so far assisted me in this work by his Spirit, that good Remembrancer; the manifestation of which, as it is minded, will help such as seriously and conscientiously read this, to find out and cleave to the truth, and also establish and confirm those who have already believed: which of all things is most earnestly desired and daily prayed for, by

ROBERT BARCLAY,
A servant of the church of Christ.

From Urie, the place of my being; in my
native country of Scotland, the 11th of
the sixth month, 1673.

CONTENTS.

A CATECHISM, &c.

CHAPTER I.

Of God, and the true and saving knowledge of him.

Q. Seeing it is a thing unquestioned by all sorts of Christians, that the height of happiness consisteth in coming to know and enjoy eternal life, what is it in the sense and judgment of Christ?

A. This is life eternal, that they might know thee the only true God, and Jesus Christ whom thou hast sent. *John* 17. 3.

Q. How doth God reveal this knowledge?

A. For God, who commanded the light to shine out of darkness, hath shined in our hearts, to give the light of the knowledge of the glory of God, in the face of Jesus Christ. 2 *Cor.* 4. 6.

Q. How many Gods are there?

A. One God. *Eph.* 4. 6.

We know that an idol is nothing in the world, and that there is none other God but one. But to us there is but one God. 1 *Cor.* 8. 4, 6.

Q. What is God?

A. God is a spirit. *John* 4. 24.

Q. Among all the blessed, glorious and divine excellencies of God, which are ascribed and given to him in the scriptures; what is that which is most needful for us to take notice of, as being the message which the apostles recorded in special manner to declare of him now under the gospel?

A. This then is the message which we have heard of him, and declare unto you, that God is light, and in him is no darkness at all. 1 *John* 1. 5.

Q. What are they that bear record in heaven?

A. There are three that bear record in heaven, the Father, the Word and the Holy Ghost; and these three are one. 1 *John* 5. 7.

Q. How cometh any man to know God the Father, according to Christ's words?

A. All things are delivered to me of my Father, and no man knows who the Son is, but the Father, and who the Father is, but the Son, and he to whom the son will reveal him. *Luke* 10. 22. *Matt.* 11. 27.

Jesus saith unto him, I am the way, the truth and the life, no man cometh unto the Father but by me. *John* 14. 6.

Q. By whom, and after what manner doth the Son reveal this knowledge?

A. But as it is written, Eye hath not seen, nor ear heard, neither have entered into the heart of man, the things which God hath prepared for them that love him, but God hath revealed them unto us by his Spirit: for the Spirit searcheth all things, yea, the deep things of God. For what man knoweth the things of a man, save the spirit of a man which is in him? even so the things of God knoweth no man, but the Spirit of God. Now, we have received, not the Spirit of the world, but the spirit which is of God, that we might know the things that are freely given to us of God. 1 *Cor.* 2. 9, 10, 11, 12.

But the Comforter, which is the Holy Ghost, whom the Father will send in my name, he shall teach you all things, and bring all things to your remembrance, &c. *John* 14. 26.

CHAPTER II.

Of the rule and guide of Christians, and of the Scriptures.

Q. Seeing it is by the Spirit, that Christ reveals the knowledge of God in things spiritual; is it by the Spirit that we must be led under the gospel?

A. But ye are not in the flesh, but in the Spirit, if so be that the Spirit of God dwell in you. Now, if any man have not the Spirit of Christ, he is none of his. For, as many as are led by the Spirit of God, they are the sons of God. *Rom.* 8. 9, 14.

Q. Is it an inward principle then, that is to be the guide and rule of Christians?

A. But the anointing, which ye have received of him, abideth in you; and ye need not that any man teach you, but as the same anointing teacheth you of all things, and is truth, and is no lie; and even as it hath taught you, ye shall abide in him. 1 *John* 2. 27.

But as touching brotherly love, ye need not that I write unto you; for ye yourselves are taught of God to love one another. 1 *Thes.* 4. 9.

Q. I perceive by this, that it is by an inward anointing and rule that Christians are to be taught: is this the very tenor of the new covenant dispensation?

A. For this is the covenant that I will make with the house of Israel, after those days, saith the Lord; I will put my laws into their mind, and write them in their hearts: and I will be to them a God, and they shall be to me a people. And they shall not teach every man his neighbour, and every man his brother, saying, Know the Lord, for all shall know me, from the least to the greatest. *Heb.* 8. 10, 11.

And they shall be all taught of God. *John* 6. 45.

Q. Did Christ then promise, that the Spirit should both abide with his disciples, and be in them?

A. And I will pray the Father, and he shall give you another Comforter, that he may abide with you for ever, even the Spirit of Truth, whom the world cannot receive, because it seeth him not, neither knoweth him: but ye know him; for he dwells with you, and shall be in you. *John* 14. 16, 17.

Q. For what end were the scriptures written?

A. For whatsoever things were written aforetime, were written for our learning, that we through patience and comfort of the scriptures might have hope. *Rom.* 15. 4.

Q. For what are they profitable?

A. Thou hast known the holy scriptures, which are able to make thee wise unto salvation, through faith which is in Christ Jesus. All scripture is given by inspiration of God, and is profitable for doctrine, for reproof, for correction, for instruction in righteousness, that the man of God may be perfect, thoroughly furnished unto all good works. 2 *Tim.* 3. 15, 16, 17.

Q. Wherein consists the excellency of the scriptures?

A. Knowing this first, that no prophecy of the scriptures is of any private interpretation. For the prophecy came not in old time by the will of man, but holy men of God spake as they were moved by the Holy Ghost. 2 *Pet.* 1. 20, 21.

Q. The scriptures are then to be regarded, because they came from the Spirit, and they also testify, that not they, but the Spirit, is to lead into all truth: in what respect doth Christ command to search them?

A. Search the scriptures, for in them ye think ye have eternal life, and they are they which testify of me. *John* 5. 39.

Q. I perceive there was a generation of old, that greatly exalted the scriptures, and yet would not believe, nor come to be guided by that the scriptures directed to: How doth Christ bespeak such?

A. Do not think that I will accuse you to the Father; there is one that accuseth you, even Moses, in whom ye trust. For had ye believed Moses, ye would have believed me; for he wrote of me. But if ye believe not his writings, how shall ye believe my words? *John* 5. 45, 46, 47.

Q. What ought such then to be accounted of, notwithstanding their pretences of being ruled by the scriptures?

A. In which are some things hard to be understood, which they that are unlearned and unstable, wrest, as they do also the other scriptures, unto their own destruction. 2 *Pet.* 3. 16.

CHAPTER III.

Of Jesus Christ being manifest in the flesh : the use and end of it.

Q. What are the scriptures which do most observably prophesy of Christ's appearance?

A. The Lord thy God will raise up unto thee a prophet from the midst of thee, of thy brethren, like unto me; unto him ye shall hearken. *Deut.* 18. 15.

Therefore the Lord himself shall give you a sign: behold a virgin shall conceive and bear a son, and shall call his name Immanuel. *Isa.* 7. 14.

Q. Was not Jesus Christ in being before he appeared in the flesh? What clear scriptures prove this, against such as erroneously assert the contrary?

A. But thou Bethlehem Ephratah, though thou be little among the thousands of Judah, yet out of thee shall he come forth unto me, that is to be ruler in Israel, whose goings forth have been from of old, from everlasting. *Mic.* 5. 2.

In the beginning was the Word, and the Word was with God, and the Word was God; the same was in the beginning with God: all things were made by him, and without him was not any thing made that was made. *John* 1. 1, 2, 3.

Jesus said unto them, Verily, verily, I say unto you, before Abraham was, I am. *John* 8. 58.

And now, O Father, glorify thou me with thine own self, with the glory which I had with thee before the world was. *John* 17. 5.

And to make all men see what is the fellowship of the mystery, which from the beginning of the world hath been hid in God, who created all things by Jesus Christ. *Eph.* 3. 9.

For by him were all things created that are in heaven, and that are in earth, visible and invisible, whether they be thrones, or dominions, or principalities, or powers; all things were created by him, and for him. *Col.* 1. 16.

God hath in these last days spoken unto us by his Son, whom he hath appointed heir of all things, by whom also he made the worlds. *Heb.* 1. 2.

Q. These are very clear, that even the world was created by Christ: but what scriptures prove the divinity of Christ, against such as falsely deny the same?

A. And the Word was God. *John* 1. 1.

Whose are the fathers, and of whom, as concerning the

2

flesh, Christ came, who is over all, God blessed for ever
Amen. *Rom.* 9. 5.

Who being in the form of God, thought it not robbery
to be equal with God. *Phil.* 2. 6.

And we know that the Son of God is come, and hath
given us an understanding that we may know him that is
true, and we are in him that is true, even in his Son Jesus
Christ: this is the true God and eternal life. 1 *John*
5. 20.

Q. What are the glorious names the scripture gives
unto Jesus Christ, the eternal Son of God?

A. And his name shall be called, Wonderful, Counsellor,
the Mighty God, the Everlasting Father, the Prince of
Peace. *Isa.* 9. 6.

Who is the image of the invisible God, the first-born of
every creature. *Col.* 1. 15.

Who being the brightness of his glory, and the express
image of his person (or more proper according to the
Greek, of his substance.) *Heb.* 1. 3.

And he was clothed with a vesture dipt in blood; and
his name is called the Word of God. *Rev.* 19. 13.

Q. After what manner was the birth of Christ?

A. Now the birth of Jesus Christ was on this wise:
when as his mother Mary was espoused to Joseph (before
they came together) she was found with child of the Holy
Ghost. *Mat.* 1. 18.

And the angel said unto her, Fear not Mary, for thou
hast found favour with God. And behold thou shalt conceive in thy womb, and bring forth a son, and shalt call
his name Jesus: he shall be great, and shall be called the
son of the Highest; and the Lord God shall give unto
him the throne of his father David. Then said Mary unto
the angel, how shall this be, seeing I know not a man?
And the angel answered and said unto her, The Holy Ghost
shall come upon thee, and the power of the Highest shall
overshadow thee: therefore also that holy thing, that shall
be born of thee, shall be called the Son of God. *Luke* 1.
30, 31, 32, 34, 35.

Q. Was Jesus Christ, who was born of the virgin Mary, and supposed to be the son of Joseph, a true and real
man?

A. Forasmuch as the children are partakers of flesh and blood, he also himself took part of the same, that through death he might destroy him that had the power of death, that is, the devil. *Heb.* 2. 14.

For verily he took not on him the nature of angels, but he took on him the seed of Abraham. Wherefore in all things it behoved him to be made like unto his brethren, that he might be a merciful and faithful high priest, &c. *Heb.* 2. 16, 17.

For we have not an high priest which cannot be touched with the feeling of our infirmities, but was in all points tempted as we are, yet without sin. *Heb.* 4. 15.

And the gift by grace, which is by one man, Jesus Christ, hath abounded unto many. *Rom.* 5. 15.

But now is Christ risen from the dead, and become the first fruits of them that slept. For since by man came death, by man came also the resurrection of the dead. 1 *Cor.* 15. 20, 21.

Q. After what manner doth the scripture assert the conjunction and unity of the eternal Son of God, in and with the man Christ Jesus?

A. And the Word was made flesh, and dwelt among us, and we beheld his glory, the glory as of the only begotten of the Father, full of grace and truth. *John* 1. 14.

For he whom God hath sent, speaketh the words of God; for God giveth not the Spirit by measure unto him. *John* 3. 34.

How God anointed Jesus of Nazareth with the Holy Ghost and with power, who went about doing good, and healing all that were oppressed of the devil; for God was with him. *Acts* 10. 38.

For it pleased the Father, that in him should all fulness dwell. *Col.* 1. 19.

For in him dwelleth all the fulness of the Godhead bodily. *Col.* 2. 9.

In him are hid all the treasures of wisdom and knowledge. *Col.* 2. 3.

Q. For what end did Christ appear in the world?

A. For what the law could not do, in that it was weak through the flesh; God sending his Son, in the likeness of sinful flesh, and for sin, condemned sin in the flesh. *Rom.* 8. 3.

For this purpose the Son of God was manifested, that he might destroy the works of the devil. And ye know that he was manifested to take away our sins. 1 *John* 3. 8, 5.

Q. Was Jesus Christ really crucified and raised again?

A. For I delivered unto you first of all, that which I also received, how that Christ died for our sins, according to the scriptures: and that he was buried, and that he rose again the third day, according to the scriptures. 1 *Cor.* 15. 3, 4.

Q. What end do the scriptures ascribe unto the coming, death and sufferings of Christ?

A. For mine eyes have seen thy salvation, which thou hast prepared before the face of all people. A light to lighten the Gentiles, and the glory of thy people Israel. *Luke* 2. 30, 31, 32.

Whom God hath set forth to be a propitiation through faith in his blood, to declare his righteousness for the remission of sins that are past, through the forbearance of God. *Rom.* 3. 25.

And walk in love, as Christ also hath loved us, and hath given himself for us, an offering and a sacrifice to God for a sweet smelling savour. *Eph.* 5. 2.

And having made peace through the blood of his cross by him, to reconcile all things unto himself; by him, I say, whether they be things in earth, or things in heaven. And you that were some time alienated, and enemies in your minds by wicked works ; yet now hath he reconciled in the body of his flesh, through death, to present you holy, unblamable and unreprovable in his sight. *Col.* 1. 20, 21, 22.

Neither by the blood of goats and calves, but by his own blood, he entered in once into the holy place, having obtained eternal redemption for us. How much more shall the blood of Christ, who through the eternal Spirit offered himself without spot to God, purge your consciences from dead works to serve the living God? *Heb.* 9. 12, 14.

For Christ also hath once suffered for sins, the just for

the unjust, that he might bring us to God, being put to
death in the flesh, but quickened by the Spirit. 1 *Pet.*
3. 18.

Hereby perceive we the love of God, because he laid
down his life for us. 1 *John* 3. 16.

And for this cause he is the mediator of the New Testament, that by means of death for the redemption of the
transgressions that were under the first Testament, they
which are called, might receive the promise of the eternal
inheritance. *Heb.* 9. 15.

Q. Is Christ then the Mediator?

A. For there is one God, and one Mediator between God
and man, the man Christ Jesus, who gave himself a ransom
for all, to be testified in due time. 1 *Tim.* 2. 5.

Q. Was not Christ the Mediator until he appeared, and
was crucified in the flesh?

A. He is the Lamb that was slain from the foundation
of the world. *Rev.* 5. 12, & 13. 8.

Q. Is it needful then to believe, that the saints of old
did partake of Christ, as then present with and nourishing
them?

A. Moreover, brethren, I would not that ye should be
ignorant, how that all our fathers were under the cloud,
and all passed through the sea, and were all baptised unto
Moses in the cloud, and in the sea, and did all eat the same
spiritual meat; and did all drink the same spiritual drink;
for they drank of that spiritual Rock that followed them,
and that Rock was Christ. 1 *Cor.* 10. 1, 2, 3, 4.

Q. But whereas most of these scriptures before mentioned, do hold forth, that the death and sufferings of Christ
were appointed for the destroying, removing, and remitting
of sin; did he so do it while he was outwardly upon earth,
as not to leave any thing for himself to do in us, nor for us
to do, in and by his strength?

A. For even hereunto were ye called, because Christ
also suffered for us, leaving us an example, that ye should
follow his steps. 1 *Pet.* 2. 21.

Whereof I Paul am made a minister, who now rejoice
in my sufferings for you, and fill up that which is behind
of the afflictions of Christ in my flesh, for his body's sake,
which is the church. *Col.* 1. 23, 24.

2 *

Always bearing about in the body the dying of the
Lord Jesus; that the life also of Jesus might be made
manifest in our body. For we which live, are alway delivered unto death for Jesus's sake, that the life also of
Jesus might be made manifest in our mortal flesh. 2 *Cor.*
4. 10, 11.

And that he died for all, that they which live, should
not henceforth live unto themselves, but unto him that died
for them, and rose again. 2 *Cor.* 5. 15.

That I may know him, and the power of his resurrection,
and the fellowship of his sufferings, being made conformable
to his death. *Phil.* 3. 10.

CHAPTER IV.

*Of the new birth, the inward appearance of Christ in spirit,
and the unity of the saints with him.*

Q. Doth Christ promise then to come again to his disciples?

A. I will not leave you comfortless; I will come unto
you. *John* 14. 18.

Q. Was this only a special promise to these disciples?
or is it not the common privilege of the saints?

A. For thus saith the high and lofty One, that inhabits
eternity, whose name is Holy; I dwell in the high and
holy place; with him also that is of a contrite and humble
spirit, &c. *Isa.* 57. 15.

For ye are the temple of the living God; as God hath
said, I will dwell in them and walk in them. 2. *Cor.* 6. 16.

Behold I stand at the door and knock; if any man hear
my voice, and open the door, I will come in to him, and
sup with him, and he with me. *Rev.* 3. 20.

Q. Doth the apostle Paul speak of the Son of God's
being revealed in him?

A. But when it pleased God, who separated me from
my mother's womb, and called me by his grace, to reveal
his Son in me, that I might preach him among the heathen. *Gal.* 1. 15, 16.

Q. Is it needful then to know Christ within?

A. Examine yourselves, whether ye be in the faith;

prove your own selves. Know ye not your own selves, how that Jesus Christ is in you ; except ye be reprobates. 2 *Cor.* 13. 5.

Q. Was the apostle earnest, that this inward birth of Christ should be brought forth in any ?

A. My little children, of whom I travail in birth again, until Christ be formed in you. *Gal.* 4. 19.

Q. What saith the same apostle, of the necessity of this inward knowledge of Christ, and of the new creature beyond the outward ?

A. Wherefore henceforth know we no man after the flesh ; yea, though we have known Christ after the flesh, yet now henceforth know we him no more. Therefore if any man be in Christ, he is a new creature ; old things are passed away, behold all things are become new. 2 *Cor.* 5. 16, 17.

But ye have not so learned Christ ; if so be that ye have heard him, and have been taught by him, as the truth is in Jesus : that ye put off, concerning the former conversation, the old man which is corrupt, according to the deceitful lusts ; and be renewed in the spirit of your mind ; and that ye put on the new man, which after God is created in righteousness and true holiness. *Eph.* 4. 20, 21, 22, 23, 24.

Q. Is this Christ within, the mystery of God and hope of glory, which the apostle preached ?

A. To whom God would make known what is the riches of the glory of this mystery among the Gentiles ; which is, Christ in you the hope of glory, whom we preach. *Col.* 1. 27, 28.

Q. Doth the apostle any where else press the putting on of this new birth ?

A. Put ye on the Lord Jesus Christ, and make not provision for the flesh, to fulfil the lusts thereof. *Rom.* 13. 14.

Q. Doth he write to any of the saints, as having put off the old, and put on the new man ?

A. For as many of you as have been baptised into Christ, have put on Christ. *Gal.* 3. 27.

Seeing that ye have put off the old man with his deeds, and have put on the new man, which is renewed in know-

ledge after the image of him that created him. *Col.* 3.
9, 10.

Q. What speaketh Christ himself, of the necessity of
this new birth?

A. Jesus answered and said unto him, Verily, verily, I
say unto thee, except a man be born again he cannot see
the kingdom of God. *John* 3. 3.

Q. Of what seed cometh this birth?

A. Being born again, not of corruptible seed, but of
incorruptible, by the word of God, which liveth and abideth
for ever. 1 *Pet.* 1. 23.

Q. What doth the apostle Paul witness of himself concerning this new life?

A. I am crucified with Christ, nevertheless I live; yet
not I, but Christ liveth in me. *Gal.* 2. 20.

Q. What is the preaching of the cross of Christ?

A. For the preaching of the cross is to them that perish,
foolishness; but unto us that are saved, it is the power of
God. 1 *Cor.* 1. 18.

Q. What effect hath this cross in the apostle? And
how much preferreth he the new creature, to all outward
and visible ordinances and observances?

A. But God forbid that I should glory, save in the cross
of our Lord Jesus Christ, by whom the world is crucified
unto me, and I unto the world: For in Jesus Christ neither
circumcision availeth any thing, nor uncircumcision, but a
new creature. *Gal.* 6. 14, 15.

Q. What speaketh Christ of the unity of the saints with
him?

A. At that day ye shall know that I am in my Father,
and you in me, and I in you. *John* 14. 20.

Abide in me, and I in you; as the branch cannot bear
fruit of itself, except it abide in the vine, no more can ye,
except ye abide in me: I am the Vine, ye are the branches;
he that abideth in me, and I in him, the same bringeth
forth much fruit; for without me ye can do nothing. *John*
15. 4, 5.

Neither pray I for these alone, but for them also which
shall believe in me through their word: that they all may
be one; as thou Father art in me, and I in thee, that
they also may be one in us; that the world may believe

that thou hast sent me. And the glory which thou gavest me, I have given them, that they may be one, even as we are one: I in them, and thou in me, that they may be made perfect in one, and that the world may know that thou hast sent me, and hast loved them as thou hast loved me. *John* 17. 20, 21, 22, 23.

Q. What saith the apostle Paul to this purpose?

A. For both he that sanctifies, and they that are sanctified, are all of one; for which cause he is not ashamed to call them brethren. *Heb.* 2. 11.

Q. What saith the apostle Peter?

A. Whereby are given unto us, exceeding great and precious promises, that by these ye might be partakers of the divine nature, having escaped the corruption that is in the world through lust. 2 *Pet.* 1. 4.

CHAPTER V.

Concerning the light wherewith Jesus Christ hath enlightened every man: the universality and sufficiency of God's grace, to all the world, made manifest therein.

Q. Wherein consists the love of God towards fallen and lost man?

A. For God so loved the world, that he gave his only begotten Son, that whosoever believeth in him should not perish, but have everlasting life. *John* 3. 16.

In this was manifested the love of God towards us, because that God sent his only begotten Son into the world, that we might live through him. 1 *John* 4. 9.

Q. What is intended here by the world? all and every man, or only a few?

A. But we see Jesus, who was made a little lower than the angels, for the suffering of death, crowned with glory and honour; that he by the grace of God should taste death for every man. *Heb.* 2. 9.

And if any man sin, we have an advocate with the Father, Jesus Christ the righteous, and he is the propitiation for our sins, and not for ours only, but also for the sins of the whole world. 1 *John* 2. 1, 2.

Q. Methinks the apostle John is very plain there, in mentioning the whole world, which must be not only the saints, but all others, seeing he distinguishes the world from himself, and all the saints to whom he then wrote : What saith Paul elsewhere in this matter?

A. Christ in you, the hope of glory, whom we preach, warning every man, and teaching every man in all wisdom, that we may present every man perfect in Christ Jesus. *Col.* 1. 27, 28.

I exhort therefore, that first of all, supplications, prayers, intercessions, and giving of thanks, be made for all men : for this is good and acceptable in the sight of God our Saviour, who will have all men to be saved, and to come to the knowledge of the truth; who gave himself a ransom for all, to be testified in due time. 1 *Tim.* 2. 1, 3, 4, 6.

Q. What is the apostle Peter's testimony in this?

A. The Lord is not slack concerning his promise, as some men count slackness, but is long-suffering to us-ward, not willing that any should perish, but that all should come to repentance. 2 *Pet.* 3. 9.

Q. Are there any more scripture passages that prove this thing.

A. Say unto them, as I live, saith the Lord God, I have no pleasure in the death of the wicked, but that the wicked turn from his way and live. *Ezek.* 33. 11.

The Lord is gracious, and full of compassion; slow to anger, and of great mercy. The Lord is good to all, and his tender mercies are over all his works. *Psalm* 145. 8, 9.

To wit, that God was in Christ, reconciling the world unto himself. 2 *Cor.* 5. 19.

Q. Seeing then by these scriptures, it appears that the love of God is held out to all, that all might have been, or may be, saved by Christ; what is to be judged of those who assert, that God nor Christ never purposed love nor salvation to a great part of mankind, and that the coming and sufferings of Christ never were intended, nor could be useful to their justification; but will and must be effectual for their condemnation, even according to God's purpose; who from their very infancy to their grave, with-

held from them all means of salvation? What saith the
scripture to such?

A. For God sent not his Son into the world to condemn the world, but that the world through him might be
saved. *John* 3. 17.

I am come a light into the world, that whosoever believeth on me, should not abide in darkness. And if any
man hear my words, and believe not, I judge him not;
for I came not to judge the world, but to save the world.
John 12. 46, 47.

Q. From what scripture then came these men to wrest
an opinion so contrary to truth?

A. For the children being not yet born, neither having
done any good or evil, that the purpose of God according
to election might stand, not of works but of him that
calleth, it was said unto her, the elder shall serve the
younger; as it is written, Jacob have I loved, but Esau
have I hated. *Rom.* 9. 11, 12, 13.

Q. I perceive in that scripture it was only said, before
the children were born, the elder shall serve the younger;
these other words (Jacob have I loved, Esau have I hated)
are mentioned out of the prophet Malachi, who wrote them
many hundred years after both were dead: doth not the
scripture mention any other cause of God's hating Esau,
than merely his decree? What saith the same apostle
elsewhere?

A. Lest there be any fornicator, or profane person, as
Esau, who for one morsel of meat sold his birth-right: for
ye know how that afterward when he would have inherited
the blessing, he was rejected. *Heb.* 12. 16, 17.

Q. But seeing that such allege, that it is because of
Adam's sin, that many, even children, are damned; doth
not the scripture aver, that the death of Christ was as large
to heal, as Adam's sin could be to condemn?

A. For if through the offence of one, many be dead,
much more the grace of God, and the gift by grace, which
is by one man Jesus Christ. Therefore as by the offence
of one, judgment came upon all men to condemnation;
even so by the righteousness of one, the free gift came
upon all men unto justification of life. *Rom.* 5. 15, 18.

Q. That proves abundantly, that Christ's death is of

sufficient extent, to make up any hurt Adam's sin brought
upon mankind : what is then the cause of condemnation ?

A. He that believeth on him is not condemned; but
he that believeth not, is condemned already, because he
hath not believed in the name of the only begotten Son of
God. *John* 3. 18.

And with all deceivableness of uprighteousness in them
that perish, because they received not the love of the
truth, that they might be saved. And for this cause God
shall send them strong delusion, that they should believe a
lie, that they all might be damned who believe not the
truth, but had pleasure in unrighteousness. 2 *Thes.* 2.
10, 11, 12.

Q. Seeing it is of a truth, according to the scripture's
testimony, that God has purposed love and mercy to all,
in the appearance of his Son Jesus Christ; is the gospel
or glad tidings of this salvation, brought nigh unto all, by
which they are put into a capacity of receiving the grace,
and being saved by it ?

A. If ye continue in the faith grounded and settled,
and be not moved away from the hope of the gospel,
which ye have heard, and which was preached to every
creature which is under heaven, whereof I Paul am made
a minister. *Col.* 1. 23.

Q. What is the gospel ?

A. I am not ashamed of the gospel of Christ ; for it is
the power of God unto salvation, to every one that believeth. *Rom.* 1. 16.

Q. Is the gospel hid ?

A. If our gospel be hid, it is hid to them that are lost,
in whom the God of this world hath blinded the minds of
them which believe not, lest the light of the glorious gospel of Christ who is the image of God should shine unto
them. 2 *Cor.* 4. 3, 4.

Q. Is the light then come into the world ? and are not
men condemned because they love it not, and not because
it is hid from them ?

A. And this is the condemnation, that light is come
into the world, and men love darkness rather than light.
John 3. 19.

Q. Why do they so ?

A. Because their deeds are evil. *John* 3. 19.

Q. Is every man enlightened by this light?

A. He was not that light, but was sent to bear witness of that light: that was the true light, which lighteth every man that cometh into the world. *John* 1. 8, 9.

Q. Doth this light discover all things?

A. All things that are reproved are made manifest by the light; for whatsoever doth make manifest, is light. *Eph.* 5. 13.

Q. Do evil men preach up this light, or mind it?

A. Every one that doth evil, hateth the light, neither cometh to the light, lest his deeds should be reproved. *John* 3. 20.

They are of those that rebel against the light. *Job* 24. 13.

Q. Do good men love it and follow it?

A. He that doeth truth, cometh to the light, that his deeds may be made manifest, that they are wrought in God. *John* 3. 21.

Q. What benefit doth redound to such as love the light, and walk in it?

A. If we walk in the light, as he is in the light, we have fellowship one with another, and the blood of Jesus Christ, his Son, cleanseth us from all sin. 1 *John* 1. 7.

Q. Doth Christ command to take heed to the light?

A. While ye have the light, believe in the light, that ye may be the children of the light. *John* 12. 36.

Q. Were the apostles commanded to turn people to the light?

A. Delivering thee from the people, and from the Gentiles, unto whom now I send thee, to open their eyes, and to turn them from darkness unto light, and from the power of Satan unto God, that they may receive forgiveness of sins, and inheritance among them which are sanctified, through faith that is in me. *Acts* 26. 17, 18.

Q. Doth this light abide with every man all his life time, in order to save, or only during the day of his visitation?

A. Yet a little while is the light with you; walk while

3

ye have the light, lest darkness come upon you. *John* 12. 35.

. Again, he limiteth a certain day, saying in David, To-day after so long a time; as it is said, To-day, if ye will hear his voice, harden not your hearts. *Heb.* 4. 7.

Q. How can it be proved, that there is a day, wherein people may know things concerning their peace, which afterwards may be hid from them?

A. And when he was come near, he beheld the city, and wept over it, saying, If thou hadst known, even thou, at least in this thy day, the things which belong unto thy peace! but now they are hid from thine eyes. *Luke* 19. 41, 42.

Q. Is there any other scripture proof of the Lord's willingness to gather a people who would not, and therefore were condemned?

A. O Jerusalem, Jerusalem! thou that killest the prophets, and stonest them which are sent unto thee: how often would I have gathered thy children together, even as a hen gathereth her chickens under her wings, and ye would not? *Mat.* 23. 37.—*Luke* 13. 34.

Then his Lord, after that he had called him, said unto him, O thou wicked servant, I forgave thee all that debt, because thou desiredst me: Shouldest not thou also have had compassion on thy fellow servant, even as I had pity on thee? and his Lord was wroth, and delivered him to the tormentors, till he should pay all that was due unto him. *Mat.* 18. 32, 33, 34.

Then Paul and Barnabas waxed bold, and said, It was necessary that the word of God should first have been spoken to you; but seeing ye put it from you, and judge yourselves unworthy of everlasting life, lo, we turn to the Gentiles. *Acts* 13. 46.

Because I have called, and ye refused; I have stretched out my hand, and no man regarded: but ye have set at nought all my counsel, and would none of my reproof: I also will laugh at your calamity, I will mock when your fear cometh. *Prov.* 1. 24, 25, 26.

And at what instant I shall speak concerning a nation; and concerning a kingdom, to build, and to plant it: if it do evil in my sight that it obey not my voice, then will I repent of the good wherewith I said I would benefit them *Jer.* 18. 9, 10.

Q. Doth God's Spirit strive then for a season, and afterwards forbear?

A. And the Lord said, My Spirit shall not always strive with man. *Gen.* 6. 3.

Q. May it then be resisted?

A. Ye stiff-necked and uncircumcised in heart and ears, ye do always resist the Holy Ghost; as your fathers did, so do ye. *Acts* 7. 51.

For the wrath of God is revealed from heaven against all ungodliness and unrighteousness of men, who hold the truth in unrighteousness. *Rom.* 1. 18.

Q. Hath God manifested to man that which may be known of himself?

A. That which may be known of God, is manifest in them; for God hath shewed it unto them. *Rom.* 1. 19.

Q. Is then this light or seed sown in the hearts of evil men?

A. And he spake many things to them in parables; Behold, a sower went forth to sow, and when he sowed, some seeds fell by the way side, &c. Some fell among stony places, &c. And some fell among thorns, &c. *Mat.* 13. 3, 4, 5, 7.

Q. Are these places, where the seed is said to have fallen, understood of the hearts of men?

A. Hear ye therefore the parable of the sower. When any one heareth the word of the kingdom, and understandeth it not, then cometh the wicked one, and catcheth away that which was sown in his heart; this is he which received the seed by the way side, &c. *Mat.* 13. 18, 19.

Q. Is this seed small in its first appearance?

A. The kingdom of heaven is like to a grain of mustard seed, which a man took and sowed in his field, which indeed is the least of all seeds. *Mat.* 13. 31, 32.

Q. Forasmuch as many understand not this, under the notion and appellation of light or seed, it being quite another dialect than the common; though I must needs confess, it is the very language of the scriptures; is there a saving manifestation of the Spirit given unto all?

A. The manifestation of the Spirit is given to every man to profit withal. 1 *Cor.* 12. 12, 7.

Q. Sure, if it be to profit withal, it must be in order to save; for if it were not useful, yea, sufficient to save, what profit could it be of? but in regard some speak of a grace that is common, and of a grace that is saving, is there such a grace common to all, as brings salvation?

A. The grace of God that brings salvation, hath appeared unto all men. *Tit.* 2. 11.

Q. That which brings salvation must needs be saving; what doth that grace teach us?

A. Teaching us, that denying ungodliness and worldly lusts, we should live soberly, righteously and godly in this present world. *Tit.* 2. 12.

Q. Certainly that which teacheth both righteousness and godliness must be sufficient; for therein consisteth the whole duty of man: What saith the apostle elsewhere of this instructor?

A. And now, brethren, I commend you to God, and to the word of his grace, which is able to build you up, and to give you an inheritance among all them which are sanctified. *Acts* 20. 32.

Q. What is the word of God?

A. The word of God is quick and powerful, and sharper than any two-edged sword, piercing even to the dividing asunder of soul and spirit, and of the joints and marrow, and is a discerner of the thoughts and intents of the heart. Neither is there any creature that is not manifest in his sight, but all things are naked and open to the eyes of him with whom we have to do. *Heb.* 4. 12, 13.

Q. Ought we to take heed to this word?

A. We have also a more sure word of prophecy, whereunto ye do well that ye take heed, as unto a light that shineth in a dark place, until the day dawn, and the daystar arise in your heart. 2 *Pet.* 1. 19.

Q. I perceive the scriptures are very clear both concerning the universality and sufficiency of this light, seed, grace and word of God; but is this word nigh or afar off, inward or outward?

A. Say not in thine heart, Who shall ascend into heaven? that is, to bring Christ down from above. Or, who shall descend into the deep? that is, to bring up Christ again from the dead. But what saith it? the word is nigh thee, in thy mouth and in thy heart; that is the word of faith which we preach. *Rom.* 10. 6, 7, 8.

Q. That is clear, as to the word; is there any scripture speaks of the light being inward?

A. God, who commanded the light to shine out of darkness, hath shined in our hearts, to give the light of the knowledge of the glory of God in the face of Jesus Christ. But we have this treasure in earthen vessels, that the excellency of the power may be of God, and not of us. 2 *Cor.* 4. 6, 7.

Q. But seeing it is also called the seed of the kingdom, is the kingdom of God also within?

A. The kingdom of God cometh not with observation; neither shall they say, lo here, or lo there; for behold, the kingdom of God is within you. *Luke* 17. 20, 21.

CHAPTER VI.

Concerning faith, justification, and works.

Q. What is faith?

A. Faith is the substance of things hoped for, and the evidence of things not seen. *Heb.* 11. 1.

Q. Is faith of absolute necessity?

A. Without faith it is impossible to please him, for he that cometh to God, must believe that he is, and that he is a rewarder of them that diligently seek him. *Heb.* 11. 6.

Q. Are we justified by faith?

A. Wherefore the law was our school-master to bring us unto Christ, that we might be justified by faith. *Gal.* 3. 24.

Q. What is the nature of this faith that availeth to justification?

A. For in Jesus Christ, neither circumcision availeth any thing, nor uncircumcision, but faith which worketh by love. *Gal.* 5. 6.

Q. Are works then necessary to justification, as well as faith?

A. But wilt thou know, O vain man, that faith without

3 *

works is dead? was not Abraham our father justified by works, when he had offered Isaac his son upon the altar? Seest thou how faith wrought with his works, and by works was faith made perfect? and the scripture was fulfilled, which saith, Abraham believed God, and it was imputed unto him for righteousness: and he was called the friend of God. Ye see then how that by works a man is justified, and not by faith only. *James* 2. 20 to 24.

Q. If then both be equally required in justification, what are those works which the apostle excludes so much?

A. By the deeds of the law, there shall no flesh be justified in his sight. *Rom.* 3. 20.

Q. But though we be not justified by the deeds of the law, is not this to exclude boasting, that the grace of God may be exalted?

A. For by grace are ye saved, through faith, and that not of yourselves, it is the gift of God; not of works, lest any man should boast, for we are his workmanship, created in Christ Jesus unto good works. *Eph.* 2. 8, 9, 10.

Q. Are even the works which are performed by grace excluded? Are we never said to be saved or justified by them?

A. Not by works of righteousness which we have done, but according to his mercy he saved us, by the washing of regeneration, and renewing of the Holy Ghost, which he shed on us abundantly, through Jesus Christ our Saviour; that being justified by his grace, we should be made heirs, according to the hope of eternal life. *Tit.* 3. 5, 6, 7.

Q. I perceive then, that to be justified by grace, is to be justified or saved by regeneration, which cannot exclude the works wrought by grace and by the Spirit; how doth the apostle add in the next verse, for the maintaining this against those that cavil about the law?

A. This is a faithful saying, and these things I will that thou affirm constantly, that they which have believed in God, might be careful to maintain good works. These things are good and profitable unto men. But avoid foolish questions, and genealogies, and contentions, and strivings about the law, for they are unprofitable and vain. *Tit.* 3. 8, 9

Q. Doth the apostle Paul, that is so much against jus-

tification by the works of the law, speak any where else
of being justified by the Spirit?

A. But ye are washed, but ye are sanctified, but ye are
justified in the name of the Lord Jesus, and by the Spirit
of our God. 1 *Cor.* 6. 11.

Q. But since the law gives not power nor ability to obey,
and so falls short of justification, is there no power under
the gospel, by which the righteousness of the law comes
to be fulfilled inwardly?

A. For what the law could not do, in that it was weak
through the flesh, God sending his own Son in the likeness of sinful flesh, and for sin, condemned sin in the flesh:
that the righteousness of the law might be fulfilled in us,
who walk not after the flesh, but after the Spirit. *Rom.*
8. 3, 4.

Q. Seeing then there is power in the Spirit, are not
works through it, a condition upon which life is proposed
under the new covenant?

A. For if ye live after the flesh, ye shall die; but if ye,
through the Spirit, do mortify the deeds of the body, ye
shall live. *Rom.* 8. 13.

Q. Do not the apostles then frequently propose life to
people, upon condition of repentance and other works?

A. Repent ye therefore, and be converted, that your
sins may be blotted out. *Acts* 3. 19.

And if children, then heirs; heirs of God, and joint
heirs with Christ; if so be that we suffer with him, that
we may also be glorified together. *Rom.* 8. 17.

It is a faithful saying: for if we be dead with him, we
shall also live with him; if we suffer, we shall also reign
with him. If a man therefore purge himself from these,
he shall be a vessel unto honour, sanctified and meet for
the master's use, and prepared unto every good work.
2 *Tim.* 2. 11, 12, 21.

Remember therefore from whence thou art fallen, and
repent, and do the first works, or else I will come unto
thee quickly, and remove thy candlestick out of his place,
except thou repent. *Rev.* 2. 5.

Q. It appears clearly by these passages, that the apostle excludes only our righteousness, which he elsewhere
explains, as being the righteousness of the law, from be-

ing necessary to justification, and not such works as the
law of the spirit of life leads to, and are not so much ours
as Christ in us; are not such good works rewarded, though
they require no absolute merit, as being the fruits of free
grace; yet doth not God judge according to them, and may
they not be said to have a reward?

A. But if a man be just, and do that which is lawful
and right, and hath not eaten upon the mountains, neither
hath lifted up his eyes to the idols of the house of Israel,
neither hath defiled his neighbour's wife, neither hath
come near to a menstruous woman; and hath not oppressed
any, but hath restored to the debtor his pledge, hath
spoiled none by violence, hath given his bread to the hun-
gry, and hath covered the naked with a garment: he that
hath not given forth upon usury, neither hath taken any
increase; that hath withdrawn his hand from iniquity,
hath executed true judgment between man and man, hath
walked in my statutes, and hath kept my judgments, to
deal truly; he is just, he shall surely live, saith the Lord
God. *Ezek.* 18. 5, 6, 7, 8, 9.

For the Son of Man shall come in the glory of his Father, with his angels, and then he shall reward every man
according to his works. *Mat.* 16. 27.

Then Peter opened his mouth and said, Of a truth I
perceive that God is no respecter of persons: but in every
nation, he that feareth him, and worketh righteousness,
is acccepted with him. *Acts* 10. 34, 35.

The righteous judgment of God; who will render to
every man according to his deeds: to them, who by patient continuance in well doing, seek for glory and honour,
and immortality, eternal life: but glory, honour and peace
to every man that worketh good, to the Jew first, and also
to the Gentile. *Rom.* 2. 5, 6, 7, 10.

For we must all appear before the judgment seat of
Christ, that every one may receive the things done in his
body, according to that he hath done, whether it be good
or bad. 2 *Cor.* 5. 10.

Which is a manifest token of the righteous judgment
of God, that ye may be counted worthy of the kingdom
of God, for which ye also suffer. 2 *Thes.* 1. 5.

But whoso looketh into the perfect law of liberty, and

continueth therein, he being not a forgetful hearer, but a doer of the work, this man shall be blessed in his deed. *James* 1. 25.

Cast not away therefore your confidence, which hath great recompense of reward. *Heb.* 10. 35.

And if ye call on the Father, who, without respect of persons, judgeth according to every man's work, pass the time of your sojourning here in fear. 1 *Pet.* 1. 17.

And behold I come quickly, and my reward is with me, to give every man according as his work shall be. Blessed are they that do his commandments, that they may have right to the tree of life, and may enter in through the gates into the city. *Rev.* 22. 12, 14.

Q. It should seem that the purpose of God, in sending his Son, the Lord Jesus Christ, was not simply to save men by an imputative righteousness altogether without them; but also by the washing of regeneration, or an inward righteousness: What saith the scripture further of this?

A. And thou shalt call his name Jesus, for he shall save his people from their sins. *Mat.* 1. 21.

Looking for that blessed hope, and the glorious appearing of the great God, and our Saviour Jesus Christ, who gave himself for us, that he might redeem us from all iniquity, and purify unto himself a peculiar people, zealous of good works. *Tit.* 2. 13, 14.

CHAPTER VII.

Concerning perfection, or freedom from sin.

Q. I perceive then by all these scriptures afore-mentioned, that Christ, as well as he hath purchased pardon for our sins, hath also obtained power by which we may even here be cleansed from the filth of them: May we expect then in this life to be freed from the dominion of sin?

A. For sin shall not have dominion over you. *Rom.* 6. 14.

Q. For what reason?

A. For ye are not under the law, but under grace.
Rom. 6. 14.

Q. How cometh the apostle then to cry out and complain of sin, saying, Who shall deliver me from the body of this death? Doth he speak that as a condition always permanent to him and other saints, or only that which he had passed through? What saith he afterwards?

A. There is therefore now no condemnation to them which are in Christ Jesus, who walk not after the flesh, but after the Spirit. For the law of the Spirit of life in Christ Jesus, hath made me free from the law of sin and death. Who shall separate us from the love of Christ? Shall tribulation, or distress, or persecution, or famine, or nakedness, or peril, or sword? (As it is written, For thy sake we are killed all the day long: we are counted as sheep for the slaughter.) Nay, in all these things we are more than conquerors through him that loved us. For I am persuaded that neither death nor life, nor angels, nor principalities, nor powers; nor things present, nor things to come, nor height nor depth, nor any other creature, shall be able to separate us from the love of God, which is in Christ Jesus our Lord. *Rom.* 8. 1, 2. 35 to 39.

Q. What saith that apostle then unto such, who taking occasion from his words, should plead for continuance in sin for term of life, and think to be saved by the imputative righteousness of Christ, as being under grace?

A. What shall we say then? Shall we continue in sin, that grace may abound? God forbid. *Rom.* 6. 1, 2.

What then? Shall we sin, because we are not under the law, but under grace? God forbid. *Rom.* 6. 15.

Q. Is not the apostle then so far from supposing that condition, of being always under sin, to be his own constant condition, or that of all the saints, that he even supposes many of the then church of Rome, to whom he wrote, to be free of it? How bespeaketh he them, as in relation to this matter?

A. How shall we that are dead to sin, live any longer therein? Know ye not, that so many of us as were baptised into Jesus Christ, were baptised into his death?

Therefore we are buried with him by baptism into death; that like as Christ was raised up from the dead by the glory of the Father, even so we also should walk in newness of life. For if we have been planted together in the likeness of his death, we shall be also in the likeness of his resurrection; knowing this, that our old man is crucified with him, that the body of sin might be destroyed, that henceforth we should not serve sin. For he that is dead, is freed from sin. Likewise reckon ye also yourselves to be dead indeed unto sin; but alive unto God, through Jesus Christ our Lord. Let not sin therefore reign in your mortal body, that ye should obey it in the lusts thereof. Neither yield ye your members as instruments of unrighteousness unto sin; but yield yourselves unto God, as those that are alive from the dead; and your members as instruments of righteousness unto God. Know ye not, that to whom ye yield yourselves servants to obey; his servants ye, are to whom ye obey, whether of sin unto death, or of obedience unto righteousness? But God be thanked, that ye were the servants of sin, but ye have obeyed from the heart, that form of doctrine which was delivered unto you; being then made free from sin, ye became the servants of righteousness. I speak after the manner of men, because of the infirmity of your flesh; for as ye have yielded your members servants to uncleanness, and to iniquity, unto iniquity; even so now yield your members servants to righteousness, unto holiness. For when ye were the servants of sin, ye were free from righteousness. What fruit had ye then in those things whereof ye are now ashamed? For the end of those things is death. But now, being made free from sin, and become servants to God, ye have your fruit unto holiness, and the end everlasting life. For the wages of sin is death, but the gift of God is eternal life, through Jesus Christ our Lord. *Rom.* 6. 2, 3, 4, 5, 6, 7. 11, 12, 13. 16 to 23.

Q. It would appear then, that God requires of us to be perfect?

A. Be ye therefore perfect, even as your Father which is in heaven is perfect. *Mat.* 5. 48.

Q. Is it then possible to keep the commandments?

A. My yoke is easy and my burthen is light. For this
is the love of God, that we keep his commandments, and
his commandments are not grievous. *Mat.* 11. 30.—
1 *John* 5. 3.

Q. Is it necessary then for salvation, to keep the commandments?

A. Blessed are they that do his commandments, that
they may have right to the tree of life, and may enter in
through the gates into the city. *Rev.* 22. 14.

Q. Do you understand by this perfection, that any have
kept the commandments, as never to have sinned?

A. If we say that we have not sinned, we make him a
liar, and his word is not in us. 1 *John* 1. 10.

Q. Do you understand, that those who are perfect may
say, they have no sin, or only that having sinned, and so
having sin, in respect they once sinned, as the apostle in
the passage cited mentions; may they notwithstanding
thereof, come to know forgiveness for the guilt, but also
cleansing from the filth?

· A. If we say we have no sin, we deceive ourselves, and
the truth is not in us: if we confess our sin, he is faithful
and just to forgive us our sins, and to cleanse us from all
unrighteousness. 1 *John* 1. 8, 9.

Q. That scripture seems to be very plain, being com-
pared with the other before mentioned: but because some
are apt to mistake and wrest the words of the apostle,
what saith he elsewhere? Did he judge any could know
God, or be true Christians, who kept not the commandments?

A. My little children, these things write I unto you,
that ye sin not; and if any man sin, we have an advocate
with the Father, Jesus Christ the righteous: and hereby
do we know that we know him, if we keep his commandments. He that saith, I know him, and keepeth not his
commandments, is a liar, and the truth is not in him. But
whoso keepeth his word, in him verily is the love of
God perfected: hereby know we that we are in him. He
that saith he abideth in him, ought himself also to walk
even as he walked. 1 *John* 2. 1, 3, 4, 5, 6.

Beloved, now are we the sons of God, and it doth not
yet appear what we shall be; but we know, that when he

shall appear, we shall be like him, for we shall see him as he is: and every man that hath this hope in him, purifieth himself even as he is pure. Whosoever committeth sin, transgresseth also the law, for sin is the transgression of the law. And ye know that he was manifested to take away our sins; and in him is no sin. Whosoever abideth in him sinneth not. Whosoever sinneth, hath not seen him, neither known him. Little children, let no man deceive you: he that doeth righteousness is righteous, even as he is righteous. He that committeth sin is of the devil; for the devil sinneth from the beginning. For this purpose the Son of God was manifested, that he might destroy the works of the devil. Whosoever is born of God, doth not commit sin; for his seed remaineth in him, and he cannot sin, because he is born of God. In this the children of God are manifest, and the children of the devil. Whosoever doth not righteousness, is not of God, neither he that loveth not his brother. 1 *John* 3. 2 to 10.

Q. It is very plain by these passages, that the apostles. were far of another mind, than those that plead for sin during term of life, and much against the deceit of those who will esteem themselves good Christians while they live in their sins.

A. Not every one that saith unto me, Lord, Lord, shall. enter into the kingdom of heaven, but he that doth the will of my Father which is in heaven. Therefore, whosoever heareth these sayings of mine, and doeth them, I will liken him to a wise man, which built his house upon a rock. *Mat.* 7. 21, 24.

If ye know these things, happy are ye if ye do them. *John* 13. 17.

Q. What saith the apostle Paul further concerning the needfulness of this thing?

A. Circumcision is nothing, and uncircumcision is nothing; but the keeping of the commandments of God. 1 *Cor.* 7. 19.

Q. Was not this, according to the apostle Paul's judgment, the very intention of Christ, to have his church and children to be pure and without spot?

4

A. According as he has chosen us in him before the foundation of the world, that we should be holy, and without blame before him in love. *Eph.* 1. 4.

Even as Christ also loved the church, and gave himself for it, that he might sanctify and cleanse it, that he might present it to himself a glorious church, not having spot or wrinkle, or any such thing, but that it should be holy and without blemish. *Eph.* 5. 25, 26, 27.

Q. Doth not Paul press the same thing further, besides the other passages above mentioned?

A. Having therefore these promises, dearly beloved, let us cleanse ourselves from all filthiness of the flesh and spirit, perfecting holiness in the fear of God. Finally, brethren, farewell; be perfect. Christ in you the hope of glory, whom we preach, warning every man, and teaching every man in all wisdom, that we may present every man perfect in Christ Jesus. Labouring fervently for you in prayers, that ye may stand perfect and complete in all the will of God. To the end he may establish your hearts unblamable in holiness before God. And the very God of peace sanctify you wholly; and I pray God, your whole spirit and soul, and body, be preserved blameless unto the coming of our Lord Jesus Christ. 2 *Cor.* 7. 1.—2 *Cor.* 13. 11.—*Col.* 1. 28.—*Col.* 4. 12.— 1 *Thes.* 3. 13.—1 *Thes.* 5. 23.

Q. Is not this then the very end for which God appointed teachers in his church?

A. And he gave some apostles, and some prophets, and some evangelists, and some pastors and teachers, for the perfecting of the saints, for the work of the ministry, for the edifying of the body of Christ, till we all come in the unity of the faith, and of the knowledge of the Son of God, unto a perfect man, unto the measure of the stature of the fulness of Christ. *Eph.* 4. 11, 12, 13.

Q. Seeing this is so much pressed by the holy men, doth not the scripture, which cannot lie, give some of the saints this testimony, as being free from sin at some times, and so not always and daily sinning, as is supposed?

A. Noah was a just man, and perfect in his generation; and Noah walked with God. And the Lord said unto Satan, Hast thou considered my servant Job, that there is none like him in the earth, a perfect and an upright man, one that feareth God, and escheweth evil. There was in the days of Herod, king of Judea, a certain priest, named Zacharias, of the course of Abia; and his wife was of the daughters of Aaron, and her name was Elizabeth; and they were both righteous before God, walking in all the commandments and ordinances of the Lord blameless. *Gen.* 6. 9.—*Job* 1. 8.—*Luke* 1. 5, 6.

Q. That proves sufficiently as to particular persons; but what doth the scripture intimate of this, even of considerable numbers?

A. But God, who is rich in mercy, for his great love wherewith he hath loved us, even when we were dead in sins, hath quickened us together with Christ, and hath raised us up together, and made us sit together in heavenly places in Christ Jesus. But ye are come unto Mount Sion, and unto the city of the living God, the heavenly Jerusalem, and to an innumerable company of angels, to the general assembly and church of the first-born, which are written in heaven, to God the judge of all, and to the spirits of just men made perfect. And I looked, and lo, a Lamb stood on Mount Sion, and with him an hundred forty and four thousand, having his Father's name written in their foreheads. These are they which were not defiled with women; for they are virgins: these are they which follow the Lamb wheresoever he goeth: These were redeemed from among men, being the first fruits unto God, and to the Lamb. And in their mouth was found no guile, for they are without fault before the throne of God. *Eph.* 2. 4, 5, 6.—*Heb.* 12. 22, 23.—*Rev.* 14. 1, 4. —*Rev.* 5. 14.

CHAPTER VIII.

Concerning Perseverance, and falling from Grace.

Q. Is it enough for a believer, to be sure that he hath once received true grace? or is there any further certainty requisite?

A. Wherefore the rather, brethren, give diligence to

make your calling and election sure; for if ye do these
things, ye shall never fall. 2 *Pet.* 1. 10.

Q. May one that hath received true grace, have ground
to fear; or suppose he can fall?

A. But I keep under my body, and bring it into subjection, lest that by any means, when I have preached to others,
I myself should become a castaway. 1 *Cor.* 9. 27.

Q. That greatly contradicteth the doctrine of such as
say, once in grace, ever in grace: But doth the apostle
Paul express this only out of an humble esteem of himself? or doth he judge or suppose the like of other
saints?

A. Take heed, brethren, lest there be in any of you an
evil heart of unbelief, in departing from the living God.
But exhort one another daily, while it is called to-day; lest
any of you be hardened through the deceitfulness of sin.
Let us labour therefore to enter into that rest, lest any man
fall after the same example of unbelief. For it is impossible for those who were once enlightened, and have tasted
of the heavenly gift, and were made partakers of the Holy
Ghost, and have tasted the good word of God, and the
powers of the world to come; if they shall fall away, to renew them again unto repentance; seeing they crucify to
themselves the Son of God afresh, and put him to an open
shame. Looking diligently, lest any man fail of the grace
of God, lest any root of bitterness springing up, trouble
you, and thereby many be destroyed. *Heb.* 3. 12, 13.—
4. 11.—6. 4, 5, 6.—12. 15.

Q. Doth he speak this only by supposition, or doth he
assert it not only possible, but certain?

A. For the time will come, when they will not endure
sound doctrine; but after their own lusts shall they heap
to themselves teachers, having itching ears. And they
shall turn their ears from the truth, and shall be turned
unto fables. 2 *Tim.* 4. 3, 4.

Q. Doth the apostle even judge it necessary to guard
such an one, as his beloved son Timothy, against this
hazard?

A. This charge I commit unto thee, son Timothy, according to the prophecies which went before on thee, that
thou by them mightest war a good warfare, holding faith

and a good conscience; which some having put away,
concerning faith have made shipwreck. For the love of
money is the root of all evil; which while some coveted
after, they have erred from the faith, and pierced themselves through with many sorrows. And their word will
eat as doth a canker; of whom is Hymeneus and Phile-
tus, who concerning the truth have erred, saying, that the
resurrection is passed already; and overthrow the faith of
some. 1 *Tim.* 1. 18, 19.—6. 10.—2 *Tim.* 2. 17, 18.

Q. Doth the apostle any where express his fears of this,
as a thing that may happen to any number of people, who
once truly received the faith of Christ?

A. Well; because of unbelief they were broken off,
and thou standest by faith. Be not high-minded, but fear.
Now the Spirit speaketh expressly, that in the latter
times some shall depart from the faith, &c. For this
cause, when I could no longer forbear, I sent to know
your faith, lest by some means the tempter have tempted
you, and our labour be in vain. *Rom.* 11. 20.—1 *Tim.*
4. 1.—1 *Thes.* 3. 5.

Q. What is the apostle Peter's mind; does he judge
that such as have known the right way, may forsake it?

A. Cursed children, which have forsaken the right way,
and are gone astray, following the way of Balaam the son
of Bosor, who loved the wages of unrighteousness; but was
rebuked for his iniquity; the dumb ass speaking with man's
voice, forbad the madness of the prophet. These are
wells without water; clouds that are carried with a
tempest, to whom the mist of darkness is reserved for ever.
For when they speak great swelling words of vanity, they
allure through the lust of the flesh, through much wanton-
ness, those that were clean escaped from them who live
in error. For if after they have escaped the pollutions of
the world, through the knowledge of the Lord and Saviour
Jesus Christ, they are again entangled therein, and overcome, the latter end is worse with them than the beginning: for it had been better for them, not to have known
the way of righteousness, than after they have known it, to
turn from the holy commandment delivered unto them.
But it is happened unto them according to the true
proverb, the dog is turned to his vomit again, and the

4 *

sow that was washed, to her wallowing in the mire. 2 *Pet.*
2. 14 to 22.

Q. Gives he any cautions to them that stand, as supposing they may fall?

A. Ye therefore, beloved, seeing ye know these things
before, beware, lest ye also being led away with the error
of the wicked, fall from your own steadfastness. 2 *Pet.*
3. 17.

Q. May a man be truly a branch in Christ, or a real
member of his body, and afterwards be cut off?

A. If any man abide not in me, he is cast forth as a
branch, and is withered. *John* 15. 16.

Q. May a righteous man then depart from his righteousness?

A. But when the righteous man turneth away from his
righteousness, and committeth iniquity, and dieth in them;
for his iniquity that he hath done, he shall die. *Ezek.* 18.
26. and 33. 13.

Q. May a believer come to such a condition in this life,
from which he cannot fall away?

A. Him that overcometh, will I make a pillar in the
temple of my God, and he shall go no more out; and I will
write upon him the name of my God, and the name of the
city of my God, which is New Jerusalem, which cometh
down out of heaven from my God, and I will write upon
him my new name. *Rev.* 3. 12.

Q. May such an one come to be assured that he is in
this condition?

A. For I am persuaded, that neither death nor life,
nor angels, nor principalities, nor powers, nor things present, nor things to come: nor height, nor depth, nor any
other creature, shall be able to separate us from the love
of God, which is in Christ Jesus our Lord. *Rom.* 8.
38, 39.

CHAPTER IX.

Concerning the Church and Ministry.

Q. What is the church?

A. But if I tarry long, that thou mayest know how thou

oughtest to behave thyself in the house of God, which is
the church of the living God, the pillar and ground of the
truth. 1 *Tim.* 3. 15.

Q. Who is the head of the church ?

A. Who hath delivered us from the power of darkness,
and hath translated us into the kingdom of his dear Son :
And he is the head of the body, the church, from which
all the body by joints and bands, having nourishment ministered and knit together, increaseth with the increase of
God. *Col.* 1. 13. and 2. 19.

Q. What kind of persons make the church ?

A. Them that are sanctified in Christ Jesus. 1 *Cor.*
1. 2.

And the Lord added to the church daily such as should
be saved. *Acts* 2. 47.

Q. Hath not Christ appointed officers in the church, for
the work of the ministry ?

A. Wherefore he saith, when he ascended up on high,
he led captivity captive, and gave gifts unto men. And
he gave some apostles, and some prophets, and some evangelists, and some pastors and teachers ; for the perfecting
of the saints, for the work of the ministry, for the edifying of the body of Christ. *Eph.* 4. 8, 11, 12.

Q. What kind of men should such as are teachers and
overseers of the church be ?

A. A bishop then must be blameless, the husband of
one wife, vigilant, sober, of good behaviour, given to
hospitality, apt to teach ; not given to wine, no striker,
not greedy of filthy lucre, but patient, not a brawler,
not covetous ; one that ruleth well his own house, having
his children in subjection with all gravity ; for if a man
know not how to rule his own house, how shall he take
care of the church of God ? not a novice, lest being lifted
up with pride, he fall into the condemnation of the devil.
Moreover, he must have a good report of them which are
without ; lest he fall into reproach, and the snare of the
devil. 1 *Tim.* 3. 2 to 7.

For a bishop must be blameless, as the steward of God :
not self-willed, not soon angry, not given to wine, no
striker, not given to filthy lucre ; but a lover of hospitality, a lover of good men ; sober, just, holy, temperate ;

holding fast the faithful word, as he hath been taught,
that he may be able by sound doctrine, both to exhort and
to convince the gainsayers. *Tit.* 1. 7, 8, 9.

Q. What is incumbent on such to do?

A. Take heed therefore to yourselves, and to all the
flock, over which the Holy Ghost hath made you overseers,
to feed the church of God. *Acts* 20. 28.

The elders which are among you I exhort, who am also
an elder, and a witness of the sufferings of Christ, and
also a partaker of the glory that shall be revealed : Feed
the flock of God which is among you, taking the oversight
thereof, not by constraint, but willingly ; not for filthy
lucre, but of a ready mind ; neither as being lords over
God's heritage, but being ensamples to the flock. 1 *Pet.*
5. 1, 2, 3.

Q. Though they be not to lord over the flock, yet is
there not a respect due to them in their place?

A. Let the elders that rule well, be counted worthy of
double honour, especially they who labour in the word and
doctrine. 1 *Tim.* 5. 17.

Q. Albeit then, among true Christians, every one that
believeth, is to have the witness in himself, being persuaded
in himself by the Spirit ; yet is there not also a real subjection to be to one another in the Lord?

A. The spirits of the prophets are subject to the prophets. 1 *Cor.* 14. 32.

Obey them that have the rule over you, and submit yourselves ; for they watch for your souls, as they that must
give account, that they may do it with joy, and not with
grief ; for that is unprofitable for you. *Heb.* 13. 17.

And we beseech you, brethren, to know them which labour among you, and are over you in the Lord, and ad-
monish you ; and to esteem them very highly in love for
their works' sake. 1 *Thes.* 5. 12, 13.

Likewise, ye younger, submit yourselves unto the elder ;
yea, all of you be subject one to another, and be clothed
with humility ; for God resisteth the proud, and giveth
grace unto the humble. 1 *Pet.* 5. 5.

Q. How ought true teachers to minister in the church?

. A. As every man hath received the gift, even so minister the same one to another, as good stewards of the

manifold grace of God. If any speak, let him speak as the oracles of God: if any man minister, let him do it as of the ability which God giveth; that God in all things may be glorified through Jesus Christ. 1 *Pet.* 4. 10, 11.

Q. I perceive then, that every true minister of the church of Christ, is to minister of the gift and grace of God, which he hath received: but some are of the judgment, that natural wisdom or parts, and human learning, are the qualifications which are of absolute necessity for a minister; but grace they judge not to be so absolutely necessary, but that one may be a minister without it: what saith the scripture in this case?

A. A bishop must be blameless, sober, just, holy, temperate. *Tit.* 1. 7, 8.

Q. Methinks it is impossible for a man to be blameless, just, holy, sober and temperate, without the grace of God: so that if these qualifications be absolutely necessary, then surely, that without which a man cannot be so qualified, must be necessary also: but what saith the scripture, as to the necessity of natural wisdom, and human learning?

A. Where is the wise? Where is the scribe? Where is the disputer of this world? Hath not God made foolish the wisdom of this world? For after that, in the wisdom of God, the world by wisdom knew not God, it pleased God by the foolishness of preaching, to save them that believe. 1 *Cor.* 1. 20, 21.

Q. It seems then, the preachings of the true ministers are not gathered together by wisdom and learning: it hath been supposed that a man must be greatly skilled in learning, to make a good sermon? What is the apostle's judgment in the case?

A. For Christ sent me not to baptise, but to preach the gospel; not with wisdom of words, lest the cross of Christ should be made of none effect. 1 *Cor.* 1. 17.

And I was with you in weakness, and in fear, and in much trembling: and my speech, and my preaching, was not with enticing words of man's wisdom, but in demonstration of the Spirit, and of power; that your faith should not stand in the wisdom of men, but in the power of God. 1 *Cor.* 2. 3, 4, 5.

Q. I perceive the apostle lays far more stress upon the demonstration and power of the Spirit in a preacher, than upon human literature: ought ministers then to preach as the Spirit teacheth them?

A. Also we speak, not in the words which man's wisdom teacheth, but which the Holy Ghost teacheth. 1 *Cor.* 2. 13.

And they were all filled with the Holy Ghost, and began to speak as the Spirit gave them utterance. *Acts* 2. 4.

Q. Is it Christ then that speaketh in and through his ministers?

A. For it is not ye that speak, but the Spirit of your Father, which speaketh in you. *Mat.* 10. 20.

For it is not ye that speak, but the Holy Ghost. *Mark* 13. 11.

. For the Holy Ghost shall teach you in the same hour, what ye ought to say. *Luke* 12. 12.

Since ye seek a proof of Christ speaking in me, which to you-ward is not weak, but is mighty in you. 2 *Cor.* 13. 3.

Q. What is the apostle's mind of that human learning, which some cry up so much, and think so needful in a minister?

A. Beware lest any man spoil you through philosophy and vain deceit; after the tradition of men, after the rudiments of the word, and not after Christ. *Col.* 2. 8.

O Timothy! keep that which is committed to thy trust, avoiding profane and vain babblings, and oppositions of science falsely so called. 1 *Tim.* 6. 20.

Q. Though true ministers speak not by the natural wisdom of men; yet, is their testimony altogether void of wisdom?

A. Howbeit, we speak wisdom among them that are perfect; yet not the wisdom of this world, nor of the princes of this world, that come to nought: but we speak the wisdom of God in a mystery, even the hidden wisdom, which God ordained before the world to our glory. 1 *Cor.* 2. 6, 7.

Q. What is the reason, that man by his natural wisdom is not capable to minister in the things of God?

A. For what man knoweth the things of a man, save the spirit of a man, which is in him? even so the things of God knoweth no man, but the Spirit of God. But the natural man receiveth not the things of the Spirit of God, for they are foolishness unto him; neither can he know them, because they are spiritually discerned. 1 *Cor.* 2. 11, 14.

Q. These scriptures do sufficiently hold forth, that the true call to the ministry is from God; that which maketh a true minister, is the gift and grace of God; that the true and effectual preaching of a faithful minister is such, as is from the inward teaching and leading of the Spirit of God: But what say the scriptures touching the maintenance of ministers?

A. Let him that is taught in the word, communicate unto him that teacheth in all good things. *Gal.* 6. 6.

If we have sown unto you spiritual things, is it a great matter if we shall reap your carnal things? If others be partakers of this power over you, are not we rather? Nevertheless we have not used this power, but suffer all things, lest we should hinder the gospel of Christ. Do ye not know, that they which minister about holy things, live of the things of the temple? and they which wait at the altar, are partakers with the altar: even so hath the Lord. ordained, that they which preach the gospel, should live of the gospel. 1 *Cor.* 9. 11 to 14.

For the scripture saith, thou shalt not muzzle the ox that treadeth out the corn; and, the labourer is worthy of his reward. 1 *Tim.* 5. 18.

Q. I perceive by these scriptures, that there lieth an obligation upon the saints, to help with outward things, such as truly minister unto them spiritual; but this seems to be voluntary: Ought not therefore true ministers to preach, whether they be sure of this or not? What saith the apostle of himself in this case; and what adviseth he others?

A. But I have used none of these things, neither have I written these things, that it should be so done unto me; for it were better for me to die, than that any man should

make my glorying void. For though I preach the gospel,
I have nothing to glory of ; for necessity is laid upon me ;
yea, woe is unto me if I preach not the gospel, for if I
do this thing willingly, I have a reward ; but if against
my will, a dispensation of the gospel is committed unto
me, what is my reward then ? verily, that when I preach
the gospel, I make the gospel of Christ without charge,
that I abuse not my power in the gospel. 1 *Cor.* 9. 15
to 18.

I have coveted no man's silver or gold, or apparel.
Yea, you yourselves know, that these hands have ministered unto my necessities, and to them that were with me.
I have shewed you all things, how that so labouring, ye
ought to support the weak, and to remember the words of
the Lord Jesus, how he said, It is more blessed to give,
than to receive. *Acts* 20. 33, 34, 35.

Q. It is observable, that the apostle every where makes
special mention among the qualifications of teachers, that
they be not given to filthy lucre : what ought we then to
think of those teachers, who will not preach without hire?
yea, that will by violence take from those who receive no
spirituals from them ? Are they like to be the ministers
of Christ? or what else saith the scripture of such?

A. Yes, they are greedy dogs, which can never have
enough ; and they are shepherds that cannot understand ;
they all look to their own way, every one for his gain from
his quarter. *Isa.* 56. 11.

Son of man, prophesy against the shepherds of Israel,
prophesy and say unto them, Thus saith the Lord God
unto the shepherds, woe be to the shepherds of Israel,
that do feed themselves : Should not the shepherds feed
the flocks? ye eat the fat, and ye clothe you with the wool,
ye kill them that are fed ; but ye feed not the flock. As
I live, saith the Lord God, surely, because my flock became
a prey, and my flock became meat to every beast of the
field, because there was no shepherd, neither did my shepherds search for my flock ; but the shepherds fed themselves, and fed not my flock. *Ezek.* 34. 2, 3. 8.

Thus saith the Lord, concerning the prophets that
make my people err, that bite with their teeth, and cry
Peace ; and he that putteth not into their mouths, they

even prepare war against him. The heads thereof judge for reward, and the priests thereof teach for hire, and the prophets thereof divine for money; yet will they lean upon the Lord, and say, Is not the Lord amongst us? none evil can come upon us. *Micah* 3. 5, 11.

Q. These are plain testimonies from the prophets; are there none such from the apostles?

A. Perverse disputings of men of corrupt minds, and destitute of the truth, supposing that gain is godliness; from such withdraw thyself. But godliness with contentment is great gain: for we brought nothing into the world, and it is certain we can carry nothing out: and having food and raiment, let us therewith be content. But they that will be rich, fall into temptation and a snare, and into many foolish and hurtful lusts, which drown men in destruction and perdition. For the love of money is the root of all evil; which, while some coveted after, they have erred from the faith, and pierced themselves through with many sorrows. 1 *Tim.* 6. 5 to 10.

For men shall be lovers of their own selves, covetous, boasters, proud, blasphemers, disobedient to parents, unthankful, unholy. 2 *Tim.* 3. 2.

For there are many unruly and vain talkers and deceivers, especially they of the circumcision, whose mouths must be stopped, who subvert whole houses, teaching things which they ought not, for filthy lucre's sake. *Tit.* 1. 10, 11.

But there were false prophets also among the people, even as there shall be false teachers among you, who privily shall bring in damnable heresies, even denying the Lord that bought them, and bring upon themselves swift destruction. And many shall follow their pernicious ways, by reason of whom, the way of truth shall be evil spoken of. And through covetousness shall they with feigned words make merchandise of you; whose judgment now of a long time lingereth not, and their damnation slumbereth not: having eyes full of adultery, and that cannot cease from sin; beguiling unstable souls; an heart they have exercised with covetous practices, cursed children, which have forsaken the right way, and are gone astray, following

5

the way of Balaam the son of Bosor, who loved the wages
of unrighteousness. 2 *Pet.* 2. 1, 2, 3, 14, 15.

Woe unto them, for they have gone in the way of Cain,
and ran greedily after the error of Balaam for reward,
and perished in the gainsaying of Core. These are mur-
murers, complainers, walking after their own lusts, and
their mouth speaketh great swelling words, having men's
persons in admiration, because of advantage. *Jude* 11.
16.

Q. Ought there to be any order in the church of God ?

A. Let all things be done decently and in order. 1 *Cor.*
14. 40.

Q. What good order is prescribed in the church concerning preachers ? Is it fit that only one or two speak ;
or may more, if moved thereunto ?

A. If any thing be revealed to another that sitteth by,
let the first hold his peace : for ye may all prophesy one
by one, that all may learn, and all may be comforted.
And the spirits of the prophets are subject to the prophets : for God is not the author of confusion, but of
peace, as in all the churches of the saints. 1 *Cor.* 14.
30 to 33.

Q. Is there any promise, that daughters as well as sons,
shall prophesy under the gospel ?

A. And it shall come to pass afterwards, that I will pour
out of my spirit upon all flesh, and your sons and your daughters shall prophesy ; your old men shall dream dreams,
your young men shall see visions. *Joel* 2. 28.

Q. Is this promise fulfilled, and to be fulfilled ?

A. But this is that which was spoken by the prophet
Joel ; And it shall come to pass in the last days, saith
God, I will pour out of my Spirit upon all flesh, and your
sons and your daughters shall prophesy ; and your young
men shall see visions, and your old men shall dream
dreams. *Acts* 2. 16, 17.

Q. Is there any such instance of old in the scriptures ?

A. And the same man had four daughters, virgins, which
did prophesy. *Acts* 21. 9.

Q. But may all women speak, or are any commanded to
keep silence in the church ?

A. Let your women keep silence in the church ; for it

is not permitted unto them to speak, but they are commanded to be under obedience, as also saith the law, and if they will learn any thing, let them ask their husbands at home; for it is a shame for women to speak in the Church. 1 *Cor.* 14. 34, 35.

Let the women learn in silence with all subjection. But I suffer not a woman to teach, or usurp authority over the man, but to be in silence. 1 *Tim.* 2. 11, 12.

Q. The first of these seems only to relate to women that have husbands: what comes of them that have none? the second speaks nothing of the church, but only that she ought not to usurp authority over the man: hath this no limitation? doth not the same apostle give directions, how women that speak, should behave themselves in the church?

A. Every man praying or prophesying, having his head covered, dishonoureth his head. But every woman that prayeth or prophesieth with her head uncovered, dishonoureth her head; for that is even all one as if she were shaven. 1 *Cor.* 11. 4, 5.

CHAPTER X.

Concerning Worship.

Q. What is the worship that is acceptable to God?

A. But the hour cometh, and now is, when the true worshippers shall worship the Father in spirit and in truth; for the Father seeketh such to worship him. God is a Spirit, and they that worship him, must worship him in spirit and in truth. *John* 4. 23, 24.

Q. Seeing prayer is a part of worship, when ought we to pray?

A. And he spake a parable unto them to this end, that men ought always to pray and not to faint. *Luke* 18. 1.

Pray without ceasing. 1 *Thes.* 5. 17.

Q. Hath God no respect to the manner of calling upon him?

A. For there is no difference between the Jew and the Greek; for the same Lord over all, is rich unto all that call upon him. *Rom.* 10. 12.

Q. Doth God hear the prayers of all that call upon him?

A. The Lord is nigh unto all them that call upon him, to all that call upon him in truth. *Psalm* 145. 18.

The Lord is far from the wicked; but he heareth the prayer of the righteous. *Prov.* 15. 29.

Now we know that God heareth not sinners; but if any man be a worshipper of God, and doth his will, him he heareth. *John* 9. 31.

And this is the confidence that we have in him, that if we ask any thing according to his will, he heareth us. 1 *John* 5. 14.

Q. After what manner doth the apostle declare he will pray?

A. What is it then? I will pray with the Spirit, and I will pray with the understanding also: I will sing with the Spirit, and I will sing with the understanding also. 1 *Cor.* 14. 15.

Q. Must we then pray always in the Spirit?

A. Praying always, with all prayer and supplication in the Spirit, and watching thereunto with all perseverance, and supplication for all saints. *Eph.* 6. 18.

Q. Since we are commanded to pray always in it, can we do it of our own selves, without the help thereof?

A. Likewise the Spirit also helpeth our infirmities; for we know not what we should pray for as we ought; but the Spirit itself maketh intercession for us, with groanings which cannot be uttered. And he that searcheth the hearts, knoweth what is the mind of the Spirit, because he maketh intercession for the saints according to the will of God. *Rom.* 8. 26, 27.

Q. I perceive, that without the leadings and help of the Spirit, prayers are altogether unprofitable. May not a man truly utter those things that are spiritual, without the Spirit's assistance?

A. Wherefore I give you to understand, that no man speaking by the Spirit of God, calleth Jesus accursed; and that no man can say, that Jesus is the Lord, but by the Holy Ghost. 1 *Cor.* 12. 3.

Q. This is strange; it seems the Spirit is much more necessary than many called Christians suppose it to be;

some of which can scarce give a good account, whether they have it, or want it : but if a man speak things true upon the matter, are they not true as from him, if spoken without the Spirit ?

A. And though they say, the Lord liveth, surely they swear falsely. *Jer.* 5. 2.

Q. It is apparent from all these scriptures, that the true worship of God is in the spirit ; and as it is not limited to a certain place, neither to any certain time, what shall we think of them that plead for the observation of certain days ?

A. But now, after that ye have known God, or rather, are known of God, how turn ye again to the weak and beggarly elements, whereunto ye desire again to be in bondage ? ye observe days, and months, and times and years. I am afraid of you, lest I have bestowed upon you labour in vain. *Gal.* 4. 9, 10, 11.

Let no man therefore judge you in meat or drink, or in respect of an holy day, or of the new moon, or of the sabbath-day, which are a shadow of things to come ; but the body is of Christ. *Col.* 2. 16, 17.

Q. Seeing it is so, may not some Christians as lawfully esteem all days alike, as others may esteem some days above another ? what rule giveth the apostle in this case ?

A. One man esteemeth one day above another ; another esteemeth every day alike : Let every man be fully persuaded in his own mind. He that regardeth the day, regardeth it unto the Lord ; and he that regardeth not the day, to the Lord he doth not regard it. He that eateth, eateth to the Lord, for he gïveth God thanks ; and he that eateth not, to the Lord he eateth not, and giveth God thanks. *Rom.* 14. 5, 6.

Q. But is it not convenient and necessary, that there be a day set apart to meet and worship God in ? Did not the apostles and primitive Christians use to meet upon the first day of the week, to make their collections and to worship ?

A. Now concerning the collection for the saints, as I have given order to the churches of Galatia, even so do ye. Upon the first day of the week, let every one of

5 *

you lay by him in store, as God hath prospered him, that there be no gatherings when I come. 1 *Cor.* 16. 1, 2.

CHAPTER XI.

Concerning Baptism, and Bread and Wine.

Q. How many baptisms are there ?

A. One Lord, one faith, one baptism. *Eph.* 4. 5.

Q. What is the baptism ?

A. The like figure, whereunto even baptism doth now save us, (not the putting away the filth of the flesh, but the answer of a good conscience towards God,) by the resurrection of Jesus Christ, who is gone into heaven, and is on the right hand of God; angels and authorities, and powers, being made subject unto him. 1 *Pet.* 3. 21, 22.

Q. What saith John the Baptist of Christ's baptism? how distinguisheth he it from his?

A. I indeed baptise you with water unto repentance; but he that cometh after me, is mightier than I, whose shoes I am not worthy to bear, he shall baptise you with the Holy Ghost, and with fire. *Mat.* 3. 11.

Q. Doth not Christ so distinguish it also?

A. And being assembled together with them, commanded them, that they should not depart from Jerusalem, but wait for the promise of the Father, which, saith he, ye have heard of me. For John truly baptised with water, but ye shall be baptised with the Holy Ghost, not many days hence. *Acts* 1. 4, 5.

Q. Doth not the apostle Peter also observe this?

A. And as I began to speak, the Holy Ghost fell on them, as on us at the beginning. Then remembered I the word of the Lord, how that he said, John indeed baptised with water; but ye shall be baptised with the Holy Ghost. *Acts* 11. 15, 16.

Q. Then it seems John's baptism must pass away, that Christ's may take place; because John must decrease, that Christ may increase.

A. He must increase, but I must decrease. *John* 3. 30.

Q. I perceive then, many may be sprinkled with, and dipped and baptised in water, and yet not truly baptised with the baptism of Christ: What are the real effects in such as are truly baptised with the baptism of Christ?

A. Know ye not, that so many of us as were baptised into Jesus Christ, were baptised into his death? Therefore we are buried with him by baptism into death, that like as Christ was raised up from the dead by the glory of the Father, even so we also should walk in newness of life. *Rom.* 6. 3, 4.

For as many of you as have been baptised into Christ, have put on Christ. *Gal.* 3. 27.

Buried with him in baptism, wherein also ye are risen with him, through the faith of the operation of God, who hath raised him from the dead. *Col.* 2. 12.

Q. I perceive there was a baptism of water, which was John's baptism, and is therefore by John himself contradistinguished from Christ's: was there not likewise something of the like nature appointed by Christ to his disciples, of eating bread, and drinking wine, in remembrance of him?

A. For I have received of the Lord, that which also I delivered unto you, That the Lord Jesus, the same night in which he was betrayed, took bread; and when he had given thanks, he brake it, and said, Take, eat; this is my body which is broken for you; this do in remembrance of me. After the same manner also he took the cup, when he had supped, saying, This cup is the new testament in my blood; this do ye, as oft as ye drink it, in remembrance of me. 1 *Cor.* 11. 23, 24, 25.

Q. How long was this to continue?

A. For as often as ye eat this bread, and drink this cup, ye do shew the Lord's death till he come. 1 *Cor.* 11. 26.

Q. Did Christ promise to come again to his disciples?

A. And I will not leave you comfortless; I will come to you. Jesus answered and said unto him, If a man love me, he will keep my words, and my Father will love him, and we will come unto him, and make our abode with him. *John* 14. 18, 23.

Q. Was this an inward coming?

A. At that day ye shall know that I am in my Father, and you in me, and I in you. *John* 14. 20.

Q. But it would seem, this was even practised by the

church of Corinth, after Christ was come inwardly : was
it so, that there were certain appointments positively
commanded, yea, and zealously and conscientiously practised by the saints of old, which were not of perpetual
continuance, nor yet now needful to be practised in the
church ?

A. If I then your Lord and master have washed your feet,
ye ought also to wash one another's feet.   For I have
given you an example, that you should do as I have done
to you.   *John* 13. 14, 15.

For it seemed good to the Holy Ghost and to us, to
lay upon you no greater burthen than these necessary
things ; that ye abstain from meats offered to idols, and
from blood, and from things strangled, and from fornication ; from which if ye keep yourselves, ye shall do well :
Fare ye well.   *Acts* 15. 28, 29.

Is any man sick among you ? let him call for the elders
of the church, and let them pray over him, anointing him
with oil in the name of the Lord.   *James* 5. 14.

Q. These commands are no less positive than the other ;
yea, some of them are asserted as the very sense of the
Holy Ghost, as no less necessary than abstaining from
fornication, and yet the generality of Protestants have
laid them aside, as not of perpetual continuance: but what
other scriptures are there, to show that it is not necessary
for that of bread and wine to continue ?

A. For the kingdom of God is not meat and drink ; but
righteousness and peace, and joy in the Holy Ghost.   *Rom.*
14. 17.

Let no man therefore judge you in meat or drink, or in
respect of an holy day, or of the new moon, or of the Sabbath days.   Wherefore if ye be dead with Christ from
the rudiments of the world ; why, as though living in the
world, are ye subject to ordinances, (touch not, taste
not, handle not : which all are to perish with the using,)
after the commandments and doctrines of men ?   *Col.* 2.
16, 20 to 22.

Q. These scriptures are very plain, and say as much
for the abolishing of this, as to any necessity, as aught
that can be alleged for the former : but what is the bread
then, wherewith the saints are to be nourished ?

A. Then Jesus said unto them, Verily, verily, I say unto you, Moses gave you not that bread from heaven, but my Father giveth you the true bread from heaven. For the bread of God is he which cometh down from heaven, and giveth life unto the world. Then said they unto him, Lord, evermore give us this bread. And Jesus said unto them, I am the bread of life; he that cometh to me shall never hunger; and he that believeth on me, shall never thirst: I am that bread of life. Your fathers did eat manna in the wilderness, and are dead. This is the bread which cometh down from heaven, that a man may eat thereof and not die. I am the living bread, which came down from heaven; if any man eat of this bread, he shall live for ever; and the bread that I will give, is my flesh, which I will give for the life of the world. The Jews therefore strove among themselves, saying, How can this man give us his flesh to eat? Then Jesus said unto them, Verily, verily, I say unto you, except ye eat the flesh of the Son of man, and drink his blood, ye have no life in you. Whoso eateth my flesh, and drinketh my blood, hath eternal life, and I will raise him up at the last day. For my flesh is meat indeed, and my blood is drink indeed: he that eateth my flesh and drinketh my blood, dwelleth in me, and I in him. As the living Father hath sent me, and I live by the Father, so he that eateth me, even he shall live by me. This is that bread which came down from heaven: not as your fathers did eat manna, and are dead; he that eateth of this bread, shall live for ever. *John* 6. 32 to 35, and 48 to 58.

CHAPTER XII.

Concerning the life of a Christian, in general, what and how it ought to be in this world.

Q. What is true religion?
A. Pure religion and undefiled is this,—To visit the fatherless and the widows in their affliction, and to keep himself unspotted from the world. *James* 1. 27.
Q. What is required of man?

A. He hath shewed thee, O man, what is good; and what doth the Lord require of thee, but to do justly, and to love mercy, and to walk humbly with thy God? *Micah* 6. 8.

But to this man will I look, even to him that is poor, and of a contrite spirit, and trembleth at my word. *Isa.* 66. 2.

Q. Doth God then require people to be Quakers, to tremble at his word? Was there any such among the saints of old?

A. Then were assembled unto me every one that trembled at the words of the God of Israel. *Ezra* 9. 4.

Now therefore let us make a covenant with our God, to put away all the wives, and such as are born of them, according to the counsel of my lord, and of those that tremble at the commandment of our God. *Ezra* 10. 3.

Q. It seems Ezra loved well, and had a high esteem of Quakers, since he would have their counsel followed : do any other of the prophets point out Quakers, or Tremblers, as God's people?

A. Hear the word of the Lord, ye that tremble at his word : your brethren that hated you, that cast you out for my name's sake, said, let the Lord be glorified ; but he shall appear to your joy, and they shall be ashamed. *Isa.* 66. 5.

And it shall be to me a name of joy, a praise and an honour before all the nations of the earth, which shall hear all the good that I do unto them ; and they shall fear and tremble, for all the goodness, and for all the prosperity that I procure unto it. *Jer.* 33. 9.

Q. The prophets promised good things then to Quakers : What becometh of those that tremble not, and are not such?

A. Hear now this, O foolish people ! and without understanding; which have eyes, and see not; which have ears, and hear not : Fear ye not me, saith the Lord ; will ye not tremble at my presence? &c. *Jer.* 5. 21, 22.

Q. Are then all God's children Quakers? And are we commanded to quake or tremble in order to our salvation, both under the law, and now under the gospel?

A. Serve the Lord with fear, and rejoice with trembling. *Psalm* 2. 11.

I make a decree, that in every dominion of my kingdom, men tremble and fear before the God of Daniel; for he is the living God, and steadfast for ever. *Dan.* 6. 26.

Work out your own salvation with fear and trembling. *Phil.* 2. 12.

Q. What be the chief commandments?

A. Thou shalt love the Lord thy God with all thy heart, and with all thy soul, and with all thy mind. This is the first and great commandment, and the second is like unto it. Thou shalt love thy neighbour as thyself. On these two commandments hang all the law and the prophets. *Mat.* 22. 37 to 40.

Q. What ought a Christian to seek after in the first place?

A. Seek ye first the kingdom of God and his righteousness, and all these things shall be added unto you. *Mat.* 6. 33.

Q. How ought Christians to behave themselves in this world?

A. But this I say, brethren, the time is short: it remaineth, that both they that have wives, be as though they had none; and they that weep, as though they wept not; and they that rejoice, as though they rejoiced not; and they that buy, as though they possessed not; and they that use this world, as not abusing it; for the fashion of this world passeth away. 1 *Cor.* 7. 29, 30, 31. '

Q. What saith the apostle Paul further, as that which is fit for Christian men and women to be found in?

A. I will therefore, that men pray every where, lifting up holy hands, without wrath and doubting. In like manner also, that women adorn themselves in modest apparel, with shame-facedness and sobriety; not with broidered hair, or gold, or pearls, or costly array; but (which becometh women professing godliness) with good works. 1 *Tim.* 2. 8, 9, 10.

Q. I observe the apostle is much against the vanity and superfluity of clothes among Christians; what saith Peter to this?

A. Whose adorning, let it not be that outward adorn-

ing of plaiting the hair, or wearing of gold, or of putting
on of apparel: but let it be the hidden man of the heart, in
that which is not corruptible; even the ornament of a meek
and quiet Spirit, which is in the sight of God of great price.
1 *Pet.* 3. 3, 4.

Q. The apostle is very plain there: but what saith the
scripture, as to respect of persons among Christians?

A. My brethren, have not the faith of our Lord Jesus
Christ, the Lord of glory, with respect of persons. For
if there come unto your assembly a man with a gold ring,
in goodly apparel; and there come in also a poor man, in
vile raiment; and ye have respect to him that weareth
the gay clothing, and say unto him, set thou here in a
good place; and say to the poor, stand thou there, or sit
here under my foot-stool: Are ye not then partial in yourselves, and are become judges of evil thoughts? Hearken
my beloved brethren, hath not God chosen the poor of
this world, rich in faith, and heirs of the kingdom, which
he hath promised to them that love him? But ye have
despised the poor. Do not rich men oppress you, and
draw you before the judgment-seats? Do they not blas-
pheme that worthy name by the which ye are called? If
ye fulfil the royal law, according to the scripture, Thou
shalt love thy neighbour as thyself, ye do well: but if ye
have respect to persons, ye commit sin, and are convinced
of the law as transgressors. *James* 2. 1 to 9.

Q. Though that be indeed sufficient to reprove the different ranks among Christians, upon the account of riches
or birth; yet is there not a relative respect among Christians, as betwixt master and servant? What admonition
gives the apostle in this case?

A. Servants, be obedient to them that are your masters, according to the flesh, with fear and trembling, in
singleness of your heart, as unto Christ: not with eye-
service, as men-pleasers, but as the servants of Christ,
doing the will of God from the heart; with good will doing service, as to the Lord, and not to men: knowing
that whatsoever good thing any man doth, the same shall
he receive of the Lord, whether he be bond or free. And
ye masters, do the same things unto them, forbearing
threatening, knowing that your master also is in heaven;

neither is there respect of persons with him. *Eph.* 6. 5 to 9.

Servants, obey in all things your masters, according to the flesh, not with eye-service, as men pleasers, but in singleness of heart, fearing God : And whatsoever ye do, do it heartily, as to the Lord, and not unto men ; knowing that of the Lord ye shall receive the reward of the inheritance ; for ye serve the Lord Christ. But he that doeth wrong, shall receive for the wrong which he hath done ; and there is no respect of persons. *Col.* 3. 22 to 25.

Masters, give unto your servants that which is just and equal, knowing that ye also have a master in heaven. *Col.* 4. 1.

Let as many servants as are under the yoke, count their own masters worthy of all honour ; that the name of God, and his doctrine be not blasphemed. And they that have believing masters, let them not despise them, because they are brethren ; but rather do them service, because they are faithful and beloved, partakers of the benefit. These things teach and exhort. 1 *Tim.* 6. 1, 2.

Exhort servants to be obedient unto their own masters, and to please them well in all things ; not answering again, not purloining, but showing all good fidelity ; that they may adorn the doctrine of God our Saviour in all things. *Tit.* 2. 9, 10.

Servants, be subject to your masters with all fear, not only to the good and gentle, but also to the froward : for this is thank-worthy, if a man for conscience toward God endure grief, suffering wrongfully : for what glory is it, if when ye be buffeted for your faults, ye shall take it patiently? but if when ye do well, and suffer for it, ye take it patiently ; this is acceptable with God, For even hereunto were ye called, because Christ also suffered for us, leaving us an example, that ye should follow his steps. 1 *Pet.* 2. 18 to 21.

Q. What good admonitions gives the scripture, as to the relation betwixt parents and children?

A. Children, obey your parents in the Lord, for this is right. Honour thy father and thy mother, (which is the

6

first commandment with promise) that it may be well
with thee, and thou mayest live long on the earth. And
ye fathers, provoke not your children to wrath; but bring
them up in the nurture and admonition of the Lord. *Eph.*
6. 1 to 4.

Children, obey your parents in all things; for this is
well pleasing unto the Lord. Fathers, provoke not your
children to anger lest they be discouraged. *Col.* 3. 20,
21.

Q. What between husbands and wives?

A. Wives, submit yourselves unto your own husbands,
as unto the Lord. For the husband is the head of the
wife, even as Christ is the head of the church; and he is
the Saviour of the body. Therefore, as the church is
subject unto Christ, so let the wives be to their own husbands in every thing. Husbands, love your wives, even
as Christ also loved the Church, and gave himself for it;
so ought men to love their wives as their own bodies;
he that loveth his wife, loveth himself. For this cause
shall a man leave his father and mother, and shall be
joined unto his wife, and they two shall be one flesh.
Nevertheless, let every one of you in particular so love
his wife, even as himself; and the wife see that she reverence her husband. *Eph.* 5. 22 to 25, and 28, 31, 33.

Husbands, love your wives, and be not bitter against
them. *Col.* 3. 19.

Likewise, ye wives, be in subjection unto your own
husbands; that if any obey not the word, they also may
without the word be won by the conversation of the
wives, while they behold your chaste conversation coupled
with fear. Likewise ye husbands, dwell with them according to knowledge, giving honour unto the wife, as unto the
weaker vessel, and as being heirs together of the grace
of life, that your prayers be not hindered. 1 *Pet.* 3.
1, 2, 7.

Q. What is the armour of a true Christian, and wherewith ought he to wrestle?

A. Put on the whole armour of God, that ye may be
able to stand against the wiles of the devil: For we wrestle
not against flesh and blood, but against principalities,
against powers, against the rulers of the darkness of this

world, against spiritual wickedness in high places. Wherefore take unto you the whole armour of God, that ye may be able to withstand in the evil day, and having done all, to stand. Stand therefore, having your loins girt about with truth, and having on the breast-plate of righteousness, and your feet shod with the preparation of the gospel of peace: Above all, taking the shield of faith, wherewith ye shall be able to quench all the fiery darts of the wicked. And take the helmet of salvation, and the sword of the Spirit, which is the word of God. *Eph.* 6. 11 to 17.

Q. What are Christians' weapons, and for what end?

A. For though we walk in the flesh, we do not war after the flesh; for the weapons of our warfare are not carnal, but mighty through God, to the pulling down of strong holds, casting down imaginations, and every high thing that exalteth itself against the knowledge of God, and bringing into captivity every thought to the obedience of Christ. 2 *Cor.* 10. 3, 4, 5.

Q. Ought strife and envy to be among Christians?

A. Who is a wise man, and endued with knowledge amongst you? let him show out of a good conversation his works with meekness of wisdom. But if ye have bitter envying and strife in your hearts, glory not, and lie not against the truth. This wisdom descendeth not from above, but is earthly, sensual, devilish. For where envying and strife is, there is confusion and every evil work. But the wisdom that is from above, is first pure, then peaceable, gentle, and easy to be entreated, full of mercy and good fruits, without partiality, and without hypocrisy. And the fruit of righteousness is sown in peace of them that make peace. *James* 3. 13 to 18.

Q. Ought wars to be among Christians? From whence proceed they?

A. From whence come wars and fightings among you? Come they not hence, even of your lusts, that war in your members? Ye lust, and have not; ye kill and desire to have, and cannot obtain; ye fight and war, yet ye have not, because ye ask not. *James* 4. 1, 2.

Q. What saith Christ even of defensive war?

A. But I say unto you, that ye resist not evil; but

whosoever shall smite thee on thy right cheek, turn to him the other also. *Mat.* 5. 39.

But I say unto you which hear, Love your enemies; do good to them which hate you : bless them that curse you, and pray for them which despitefully use you. And unto him that smiteth thee on the one cheek, offer also the other; and him that taketh away thy cloak, forbid not to take thy coat also. *Luke* 6. 27 to 29.

Q. What saith the apostles?

A. Recompense to no man evil for evil. *Rom.* 12. 17.

Not rendering evil for evil, or railing for railing; but contrarywise, blessing; knowing that ye are thereunto called, that ye should inherit a blessing. 1 *Pet.* 3. 9.

See that none render evil for evil unto any man; but ever follow that which is good, both among yourselves, and to all men. 1 *Thes.* 5. 15.

Q. It was lawful of old to swear; and an oath for confirmation was to them an end of all strife : Is it not lawful for Christians also to swear?

A. Again, ye have heard that it hath been said by them of old time, Thou shalt not forswear thyself, but shalt perform unto the Lord thine oaths. But I say unto you, Swear not at all; neither by heaven, for it is God's throne; nor by the earth, for it is his footstool; neither by Jerusalem, for it is the city of the great King: neither shalt thou swear by thy head, because thou canst not make one hair white or black. But let your communication be yea, yea; nay, nay; for whatsoever is more than these, cometh of evil. *Mat.* 5. 33 to 37.

But above all things, my brethren, swear not; neither by heaven, neither by the earth, neither by any other oath; but let your yea be yea, and your nay, nay; lest ye fall into condemnation. *James* 5. 12.

Q. Is it fit for Christians or believers to receive carnal and worldly honour one from another?

A. How can ye believe which receive honour one of another, and seek not the honour that cometh from God only? *John* 5. 44.

Q. Doth God allow us to give flattering titles to men?

A. Let me not, I pray you, accept any man's person; neither let me give flattering titles unto man; for I know

not to give flattering titles; in so doing my Maker would
soon take me away. *Job* 32. 21, 22.

Q. What should we say to such as quarrel with us for
speaking proper sound words, as *thou* to one, *you* to
many; which is Christ's and the saints' language in the
scripture?

A. If any man teach otherwise, and consent not to
wholesome words, even the words of our Lord Jesus Christ,
and to the doctrine which is according to godliness; he is
proud, knowing nothing, but doting about questions and
strifes of words, whereof cometh envy, strife, railings, evil-
surmisings. 1 *Tim.* 6. 3, 4.

Hold fast the form of sound words, which thou hast
heard of me, in faith and love, which is in Christ Jesus.
2 *Tim.* 1. 13.

Q. What is the great commandment given by Christ to
his disciples, as that which even declareth them to be such,
and is also pressed by his apostles?

A. A new commandment I give unto you, that ye love
one another; as I have loved you, that ye also love one another. By this shall all men know that ye are my disciples, if ye have love one to another. *John* 13. 34, 35.

This is my commandment, that ye love one another, as
I have loved you. These things I command you, that ye
love one another. *John* 15. 12, 17.

Be ye therefore followers of God, as dear children; and
walk in love, as Christ also hath loved us, and hath given
himself for us, an offering and a sacrifice to God for a
sweet smelling savour. *Eph.* 5. 1, 2.

If any man say, I love God, and hateth his brother, he
is a liar; for he that loveth not his brother whom he hath
seen, how can he love God whom he hath not seen? and
this commandment have we from him, that he who loveth
God, loveth his brother also. 1 *John* 4. 20, 21.

Q. Is humility very needful to Christians? like what
must we be ere we can enter the kingdom?

A. And Jesus, said, Verily, I say unto you, except ye
be converted, and become as little children, ye shall not
enter into the kingdom of heaven. Whosoever therefore
shall humble himself as this little child, the same is greatest in the kingdom of heaven. *Mat.* 18. 3, 4..

6 *

Q. Ought Christians to lord over one another? what rule giveth Christ in this case?

A. But Jesus called them unto him and said, Ye know that the princes of the Gentiles exercise dominion over them; and they that are great, exercise authority upon them. But it shall not be so among you; but whosoever will be great among you, let him be your minister. And whosoever will be chief among you, let him be your servant. Even as the Son of man came not to be ministered unto, but to minister, and to give his life a ransom for many. *Mat.* 20. 25 to 28.

Q. How then are Christians in this world?

A. Behold I send you forth as sheep in the midst of wolves; be ye therefore wise as serpents, and harmless as doves. *Mat.* 10. 16.

Go your ways; behold, I send you forth as lambs among wolves. *Luke* 10. 3.

Q. Are we then to expect affliction and persecution here?

A. And ye shall be hated of all men for my name's sake; but he that endureth to the end shall be saved. *Mat.* 10. 42.—*Mark* 13. 13.

And ye shall be hated of all men for my name's sake. *Luke* 21. 17.

If the world hate you, ye know that it hated me before it hated you; if ye were of the world, the world would love his own; but because ye are not of the world, but I have chosen you out of the world, therefore the world hateth you. *John* 15. 18, 19.

These things I have spoken unto you, that in me ye might have peace. In the world ye shall have tribulation; but be of good cheer, I have overcome the world. *John* 16. 33.

And all that will live godly in Christ Jesus shall suffer persecution. 2 *Tim.* 3. 12.

Q. Ought we then to fear persecution?

A. Fear them not which kill the body, but are not able to kill the soul; but rather fear him who is able to destroy both soul and body in hell. *Mat.* 10. 28.

And I say unto you, my friends, be not afraid of them that kill the body, and after that, have no more that they can do. But I will forewarn you whom ye shall fear;

Fear him which after he hath killed, hath power to cast into hell, yea, I say unto you, fear him. *Luke* 12. 4, 5.

Q. What advantage is to them that suffer persecution cheerfully, and hazard to them that shun it?

A. Blessed are they which are persecuted for righteousness sake, for theirs is the kingdom of heaven. *Mat.* 5. 10.

But if ye suffer for righteousness sake, happy are ye; and be not afraid of their terror, neither be troubled. 1 *Pet.* 3. 14.

Whosoever therefore shall confess me before men, him will I confess also before my Father which is in heaven. But whosoever shall deny me before men, him will I also deny before my Father which is in heaven. He that loveth father or mother more than me, is not worthy of me. And he that taketh not his cross, and followeth after me, is not worthy of me. He that findeth his life shall lose it, and he that loseth his life for my sake shall find it. *Mat.* 10. 32, 33, 37 to 39.

Also, I say unto you, Whosoever shall confess me before men, him shall the Son of man also confess before the angels of God. But he that denies me before men, shall be denied before the angels of God. *Luke* 12. 8, 9.

Then saith Jesus unto his disciples, If any man will come after me, let him deny himself, and take up his cross, and follow me. For whosoever will save his life shall lose it; and whosoever will lose his life for my sake shall find it. *Mat.* 16. 24, 25.

If we suffer, we shall also reign with him; if we deny him, he also will deny us. 2 *Tim.* 2. 12.

If any man come to me, and hate not his father and mother, and wife and children, and brethren and sisters, yea, and his own life, he cannot be my disciple. *Luke* 14. 26.

And he said to them all, If any man will come after me, let him deny himself, and take up his cross daily and follow me. For whosoever will save his life, shall lose it; but whosoever will lose his life for my sake, the same shall save it. *Luke* 9. 23, 24.

And when he had called the people to him, with his disciples also, he said unto them, Whosoever will come after me, let him deny himself, and take up his cross and

follow me.   For whosoever will save his life, shall lose it ·
but whosoever shall lose his life, for my sake and the gospel's, the same shall save it.   *Mark* 8. 34, 35.

Q. There is nothing more certain, according to these
scriptures, than that Christians must suffer persecution in
this world, even in their persons and estates; but shall they
not also suffer in their good names, in being accounted
blasphemers, hereticks and deceivers?

A. The disciple is not above his master, nor the servant above his lord.   It is enough for the disciple, that
he be as his master, and the servant, as his lord: if they
have called the master of the house Beelzebub; how much
more shall they call them of his household? *Mat.* 10.
24, 25.

Blessed are ye when men shall revile you, and persecute
you, and shall say all manner of evil against you falsely
for my sake.   *Mat.* 5. 11.

Then they suborned men which said, We have heard
him speak blasphemous words against Moses, and against
God.   And they stirred up the people, and the elders, and
the scribes, and came upon him, and caught him, and
brought him to the council.   *Acts* 6. 11, 12.

And when they found them not, they drew Jason and
certain brethren, to the rulers of the city, crying, These
that have turned the world upside down, are come hither
also.   *Acts* 17. 6.

But this I confess unto thee, that after the way, which
they call heresy, so worship I the God of my fathers; believing all things which are written in the law and the
prophets.   *Acts* 24, 14.

Being defamed, we entreat; we are made as the filth
of the world, and are the off-scouring of all things unto
this day. 1 *Cor.* 4. 13.

By honour and dishonour, by evil report and good report, as deceivers, and yet true. 2 *Cor.* 6. 8.

Q. It is easily apparent from what is mentioned, that
Christians are to expect persecution and tribulation; and
that they are always the sheep, and never the wolves; the
persecuted, and never the persecutors; the afflicted, and
not the afflicters; the reproached, and not the reproach-
ers: Is it not fit then that Christians be so far from per-

secuting others, that they ought to pray for their persecutors? Is this Christ's command?

A. But I say unto you, love your enemies; bless them that curse you, do good to them that hate you, and pray for them which despitefully use you and persecute you. *Mat.* 5. 44.

Q. Was this Christ's own practice?

A. Then said Jesus, Father, forgive them, for they know not what they do, &c. *Luke* 23. 34.

Q. Is Christ herein to be our example?

A. For even hereunto were ye called, because Christ also suffered for us, leaving us an example, that ye should follow his steps, who did no sin, neither was guile found in his mouth: who when he was reviled, reviled not again; when he suffered, he threatened not, but committed himself unto him that judgeth righteously. 1 *Pet.* 2. 21, 22, 23.

Q. Is there an instance of any saint in scripture who followed his example herein?

A. And he kneeled down, and cried, with a loud voice, Lord, lay not this sin to their charge, &c. *Acts* 7. 60.

Q. It appears by all these scriptures, that Christianity consisteth in the exercise of fear and trembling, humility, patience and self-denial: What ought we then to think of such who place much of their religion in abstaining from marriage, and certain meats; worshipping of angels, and other such acts of voluntary humility?

A. Now the Spirit speaketh expressly, that in the latter times some shall depart from the faith, giving heed to seducing spirits, and doctrines of devils; speaking lies in hypocrisy; having their conscience seared as with a hot iron, forbidding to marry, and commanding to abstain from meats, which God hath created to be received with thanksgiving of them which believe and know the truth. 1 *Tim.* 4. 1, 2, 3.

Let no man beguile you of your reward, in a voluntary humility, and worshipping of angels, intruding into those things which he hath not seen, vainly puffed up by his fleshly mind. *Col.* 2. 18.

CHAPTER XIII.

Concerning Magistracy.

Q. What is the duty of a magistrate?

A. The God of Israel said, the Rock of Israel spake to me: He that ruleth over men must be just, ruling in the fear of God. 2 *Sam.* 23. 3.

Q. What do the scriptures speak of the duty of such as are under authority?

A. Let every soul be subject to the higher powers; for there is no power but of God: the powers that be, are ordained of God. Whosoever therefore resists the power, resists the ordinance of God; and they that resist, shall receive to themselves damnation. For rulers are not a terror to good works, but to the evil. Wilt thou then not be afraid of the power? do that which is good, and thou shalt have praise of the same; for he is the minister of God to thee for good. But if thou do that which is evil, be afraid; for he beareth not the sword in vain: for he is the minister of God, a revenger to execute wrath upon him that doth evil. Wherefore ye must needs be subject, not only for wrath, but also for conscience sake. *Rom.* 13. 1 to 5.

Submit yourselves to every ordinance of man for the Lord's sake; whether it be to the king, as supreme; or unto governors, as unto them that are sent by him, for the punishment of evil doers, and for the praise of them that do well. For so is the will of God, that with well doing ye may put to silence the ignorance of foolish men. 1 *Pet.* 2. 13 to 15.

Q. Ought tribute to be paid to them?

A. For, for this cause pay ye tribute also; for they are God's ministers, attending continually upon this very thing. Render therefore to all their dues; tribute to whom tribute is due, custom to whom custom, fear to whom fear, honour to whom honour. *Rom.* 13. 6, 7.

Then saith he unto them, Render therefore unto Cæsar the things which are Cæsar's, and unto God the things that are God's. *Mat.* 22. 21.

Q. Are we obliged to obey magistrates in such things as we are persuaded in our minds are contrary to the commands of Christ?

A. And they called them, and commanded them not to speak at all, nor teach in the name of Jesus. But Peter and John answered and said unto them, Whether it be right in the sight of God, to hearken unto you more than unto God, judge ye. For we cannot but speak the things which we have seen and heard. *Acts* 4. 18 to 20.

And when they had brought them, they set them before the council; and the high priest asked them, saying, Did not we straitly command you, that ye should not teach in this name? and behold, ye have filled Jerusalem with your doctrine, and intend to bring this man's blood upon us. Then Peter and the other apostles answered and said, We ought to obey God rather than men. *Acts* 5. 27, 28, 29.

Q. What ought to be magistrates' behaviour in such cases, according to the counsel of wise Gamaliel?

A. Then stood there up one in the council, a Pharisee, named Gamaliel, a doctor of the law, had in reputation among all the people, and commanded to put the apostles forth a little space, and said unto them, Ye men of Israel, take heed to yourselves, what ye intend to do, as touching these men. And now I say unto you, refrain from these men, and let them alone; for if this counsel, or this work, be of men, it will come to nought: but if it be of God, ye cannot overthrow it, lest haply ye be found even to fight against God. *Acts* 5. 34, 35, 38, 39.

Q. What command giveth Christ to his people under the gospel, in relation to this matter? how doth he hold forth their duty under the parable of the tares?

A. So the servants of the householder came and said unto him, Sir, didst thou not sow good seed in thy field? From whence then hath it tares? He said unto them, An enemy hath done this. The servants said unto him, Wilt thou then that we go and gather them up? but he said, Nay; lest while ye gather up the tares, ye root up also the wheat with them. *Mat.* 13. 27, 28, 29.

Q. Doth he explain these tares, of the wicked, whom the godly must not take upon them to cut off, lest through mistake they hurt the good ; but leave it to God, to do it by his angels ?

A. The field is the world ; the good seed are the children of the kingdom; but the tares are the children of the wicked one : the enemy that sowed them is the devil ; the harvest is the end of the world, and the reapers are the angels. As therefore the tares are gathered and burnt in the fire, so shall it be in the end of this world. The Son of man shall send forth his angels, and they shall gather out of his kingdom all things that offend, and them which do iniquity. *Mat.* 13. 38 to 41.

CHAPTER XIV.

Concerning the Resurrection.

Q. What saith the scripture of the resurrection of the dead ?

A. And have hope towards God, which they themselves also allow, that there shall be a resurrection of the dead, both of the just and unjust. *Acts* 24. 15.

Q. To what different end shall the good be raised from the bad, and how are they thereunto reserved ?

A. Marvel not at this, for the hour is coming, in the which all that are in the graves shall hear his voice, and shall come forth ; they that have done good, unto the resurrection of life ; and they that have done evil, unto the resurrection of damnation. *John* 5. 28, 29.

But the heavens and the earth, which are now, by the same word are kept in store, reserved unto fire, against the day of judgment, and perdition of ungodly men. 2 *Pet.* 3. 7.

Q. What must be answered to such as ask, how the dead are raised, and with what body ?

A. Thou fool, that which thou sowest is not quickened except it die. And that which thou sowest, thou sowest not that body that shall be, but bare grain, it may chance of wheat, or of some other grain. But God giveth it a body as it hath pleased him, and to every seed his own body. All flesh is not the same flesh ; but there is one kind of flesh of men, another flesh of beasts, another of

fishes, and another of birds.   There are also celestial
bodies, and bodies. terrestrial ; but the glory of the celestial is one, and the glory of the terrestrial is another.
There is one glory of the sun, and another glory of the
moon, and another glory of the stars ; for one star dif-
fereth from another star in glory.   So also is the resurrection of the dead.   It is sown in corruption, it is raised
in incorruption : it is sown in dishonour, it is raised in
glory : it is sown in weakness, it is raised in power ; it is
sown a natural body, it is raised a spiritual body.   There
is a natural body, and there is a spiritual body.   1 *Cor.*
15. 36 to 44.

Q. The apostle seems to be very positive, that it is not
that natural body, which we now have, that shall rise ; but
a spiritual body.

A. Now this I say, brethren, that flesh and blood cannot inherit the kingdom of God ; neither doth corruption
inherit incorruption.   Behold I show you a mystery ; we
shall not all sleep, but we shall all be changed in a mo-
ment, in the twinkling of an eye, at the last trump ; for
the trumpet shall sound, and the dead shall be raised incorruptible, and we shall be changed.   For this corruptible
must put on incorruption ; and this mortal must put on
immortality.   So when this corruptible shall have put on
incorruption, and this mortal shall have put on immortality, then shall be brought to pass the saying that is
written, Death is swallowed up in victory ; O Death,
where is thy sting ? O Grave, where is thy victory ?   1
Cor. 15. 50 to 55.

7

CHAPTER XV.

A short introduction to the Confession of Faith.

Having thus largely and evidently performed the chief part of that which I promised in this treatise, in giving a full account of our principles in plain scripture words, and also answering by the scriptures the chief and main objections made against us, I come to a confession of faith, in which I shall not be so large; for that I judge it not convenient to make an inter-repetition of all the scriptures before mentioned, which if needful, the reader may easily observe, were not very difficult to do. But whereas a confession of faith calleth rather for an affirmative account of one's own faith, than for the solution of objections, or any thing of debate in a discursive way, which is both more properly and pertinently performed in a catechism; therefore I have here only done so. I am necessitated sometimes to intermix some words for coherence of the matter, as sometimes (and,) and sometimes (therefore,) and the like; but not such as any ingenuous person can affirm, do add to the matter; or that may anywise justly be reckoned a comment or meaning: and therefore to avoid the censure of the most curious carping critic, these are marked with a different character. Likewise, unless I should have ridiculously offered to publish incongruous grammar, there was a true need sometimes to change the mood and person of a verb: in all which places, whosoever will look to the words, shall find it is done upon no design to alter any whit the naked import of them: as for instance, where Christ says, I am the light of the world: were it proper for me to write thus, I am the light, &c.? or can it be reckoned any whit contradicting my purpose or promise to write, Christ is the light, where the first person is changed to the third; also, sometimes I express things which are necessarily understood, as when any of the apostles say, *we;* there, instead of *we*, I write apostles; and where they say *you*, speaking to the saints; there I mention *saints* instead of it, for the connexion of the sentence sometimes requires it; as in the first article, in mentioning that of 1 John 1. 5. concerning God's being light, and in such like cases, which I know no impartial reader would have quarrelled with, though wanting this apology, which I judged meet to premise, knowing there is a generation, who when they cannot find any real or substantial ground against truth and its followers, will be cavilling at such little niceties; therefore such may see this objection is obviated.

CHAPTER XVI.

A CONFESSION OF FAITH.

CONTAINING XXIII ARTICLES.

ARTICLE I.

Concerning GOD, and the true and saving knowledge of Him.

There is one God.[1] *Who* is a spirit.[2] *And* this is the message which the *apostles heard* of him, and declared unto the *saints*, that he is light, and in him is no darkness at all.[3] There are three that bear record in heaven, the Father, the Word, and the Holy Ghost, and these three are one.[4] The Father is in the Son, and the Son is in the Father.[5] No man knoweth the Son, but the Father; neither knoweth any man the Father, but the Son, and he to whomsoever the Son will reveal him.[6] The Spirit searcheth all things, yea the deep things of God.[7] For the things of God knoweth no man but the Spirit of God: now the *saints* have received not the spirit of the world, but the Spirit which is of God, that *they might* know the things which are freely given *them* of God.[8] For the Comforter, which is the Holy Ghost, whom the Father sends in *Christ's* name, he teacheth them all things, and bringeth all things to their remembrance.[9]

ARTICLE II.

Concerning the Guide and Rule of Christians.

Christ prayed to the Father, and he *gave the saints* another Comforter, that *was* to abide with *them* for ever,

---

(1) Eph. 4. 6.—1 Cor. 8. 4. 6.　　(2) John 4. 24.　　(3) 1 John 1. 5.　　(4) Ch. 5. 7.　　(5) John 10. 38. and 14. 10, 11, and 5. 26.　　(6) Mat. 11. 27. Luke 10. 22.　　(7) 1 Cor. 2. 10. (8) 1 Cor. 2. 11, 12.　　(9) John 14. 26.

even the Spirit of Truth, whom the world cannot receive, because it seeth him not, nor knoweth him; but the saints know him; for he dwelleth with *them*, and is to be in *them*.[1] Now if any man have not the Spirit of Christ, he is none of his: For as many as are led by the Spirit of God, they are the sons of God.[2] For this is the covenant that *God hath made* with the house of *Israel, he hath* put his laws in their mind, and writ them in their hearts; and they are all taught of God.[3] *And* the anointing, which *they* have received of him, abideth in *them*; and *they* need not that any man teach *them*, but as the same anointing teacheth *them* of all things, and is truth, and is no lie.[4]

ARTICLE III.

Concerning the Scriptures.

Whatsoever things were written aforetime, were written for our learning, that we through patience and comfort of the scriptures might have hope.[5] Which are able to make wise unto salvation, through faith which is in Christ Jesus: All scripture *being* given by inspiration of God, and is profitable for doctrine, for reproof, for correction, for instruction in righteousness, that the man of God may be perfect, thoroughly furnished unto all good works.[6] No prophecy of the scripture is of any private interpretation; for the prophecy came not in old time by the will of man, but holy men of God spake as they were moved by the Holy Ghost.[7]

ARTICLE IV.

Concerning the Divinity of Christ, and his being from the Beginning.

In the beginning was the Word, and the Word was with God, and the Word was God; the same was in the be-

---

(1) John 14. 16, 17.   (2) Rom. 8. 9, 14.   (3) Heb. 8. 10, 11.
(4) 1 John 2. 27.   (5) Rom. 15. 4.   (6) 2 Tim. 3. 15, 16, 17.
(7) 2 Pet. 1. 20, 21.

7 *

ginning with God; all things were made by him, and
without him was not any thing made that was made.[1]
Whose goings forth have been from of old, from everlasting.[2] For God created all things by Jesus Christ.[3] Who
being in the form of God, thought it not robbery to be
equal with God.[4] And his name is called Wonderful,
Counsellor, the Mighty God, the Everlasting Father, the
Prince of Peace.[5] Who is the image of the invisible God,
the first-born of every creature.[6] The brightness of the
Father's glory, and the express image of his substance.[7]
Who was clothed with a vesture dipt in blood; and his name
is called the Word of God.[8] In him dwelleth all the fulness
of the Godhead bodily.[9] And in him are hid all the treasures of wisdom and knowledge.[10]

ARTICLE V.

Concerning his Appearance in the Flesh.

The Word was made flesh.[11] For he took not on him
the nature of angels; but he took on him the seed of Abraham, being in all things made like unto his brethren.[12]
Touched with a feeling of our infirmities; and in all things
tempted, like as we are, yet without sin.[13] He died for our
sins, according to the scriptures; and he was buried, and
he rose again the third day, according to the scriptures.[14]

ARTICLE VI.

Concerning the End and Use of that Appearance.

God sent his own Son in the likeness of sinful flesh,
and for sin condemned sin in the flesh.[15] For this purpose the Son of God was manifested, that he might de-

---

(1) John 1. 1, 2, 3.   (2) Micah 5. 2.   (3) Eph. 3. 9.
(4) Phil. 2. 6.   (5) Isa. 9. 6.   (6) Col. 1. 15.   (7) Heb. 1. 3.
(8) Rev. 19. 13.   (9) Col. 2. 9.   (10) Ver. 3.   (11) John 1. 14.
(12) Heb. 2. 16, 17.   (13) Ch. 4. 15.   (14) 1 Cor. 15. 3, 4.
(15) Rom. 8. 3.

stroy the works of the devil.[1] *Being manifested* to take away our sins.[2] *For* he gave himself for us, an offering and a sacrifice to God for a sweet smelling savour.[3] Having obtained eternal redemption for us.[4] *And* through the eternal Spirit offered himself without spot unto God *to* purge *our* consciences from dead works, to serve the living God.[5] He was the Lamb that was slain from the foundation of the world.[6] Of *whom* the fathers did all drink; for they drank of that spiritual Rock that followed them, and that Rock was Christ.[7] Christ also suffered for us, leaving us an example, that *we* should follow his steps.[8] *For we are* to bear about in the body, the dying of the Lord Jesus, that the life also of Jesus might be made manifest in our body, *being* alway delivered unto death for Jesus's sake, that the life also of Jesus *may* be made manifest in our flesh.[9] That *we* may know him, and the power of his resurrection, and the fellowship of his sufferings, being made conformable to his death.[10]

ARTICLE VII.

Concerning the inward manifestation of Christ.

God *dwelleth* with the contrite and humble in spirit.[11] *For* he hath said, *He* will dwell in them and walk in them.[12] *And Christ standeth* at the door, and *knocketh ;* if any man hear *his* voice, and open the door, *he* will come in to him, and sup with him, and he with *him.*[13] *And therefore ought we* to examine *our* selves, and prove *our* own selves, knowing how that Christ is in *us* except *we* be reprobates.[14] *For* this is the riches of the glory of *the* mystery, which God would make known among (*or rather IN*) the *Gentiles,* Christ in you, the hope of glory.[15]

---

(1) 1 John 3. 8.   (2) Ver. 5.   (3) Eph. 5. 2.   (4) Heb. 9. 12. (5) Ver. 14.   (6) Rev. 5. 8, & 12, 13. 8.   (7) 1 Cor. 10. 1 to 4. (8) 1 Pet, 2. 21,   (9) 2 Cor. 4. 10, 11.   (10) Phil. 3. 10.   (11) Isa. 57. 15.   (12) 2 Cor. 6. 16.   (13) Rev. 3. 20.   (14) 2 Cor. 13. 5. (15) Col. 1. 27.

ARTICLE VIII.

Concerning the New-Birth.

Except a man be born again, he cannot see the kingdom of God.[1] *Therefore ought we* to put off the old man with his deeds, and put on the new man, which is renewed in knowledge after the image of him that created him, and which after God is created in righteousness and true holiness.[2] For henceforth know we no man after the flesh; yea, though we have known Christ after the flesh, yet now henceforth know we him no more.[3] For if any man be in Christ, he is a new creature, old things are passed away; behold, all things are become new.[4] *For such have* put on the Lord Jesus Christ.[5] And are renewed in the spirit of *their* minds.[6] *For* as many as have been baptised into Christ, have put on Christ.[7] Being born again, not of corruptible seed, but of incorruptible, by the word of God, which liveth and abideth for ever.[8] *And* glory *in nothing*, save in the cross of the Lord Jesus Christ, by whom the world is crucified unto *them*, and *they* unto the world.[9] For in Christ Jesus, neither circumcision availeth any thing, nor uncircumcision, but a new creature.[10]

ARTICLE IX.

Concerning the unity of the Saints with Christ.

He that sanctifieth, and they who are sanctified, are all of one.[11] *For* by the exceeding great and precious promises that are given them, *they are made* partakers of the divine nature.[12] *Because for this end prayed Christ, they* all might be one, as *the* Father *is* in *him*, and *he* in *the Father*, that they also *might* be one in *them;* and the glory which *he had gotten from the Father*, he gave them, that they might be one, even as the *Father* and *he* is one;

(1) John 3. 3. (2) Eph. 4. 23, 24. Col. 3. 10. (3) 2 Cor. 5. 16. (4) Ver. 17. (5) Rom. 13. 14. (6) Eph. 4. 23. (7) Gal. 3. 27. (8) 1 Pet. 1. 23. (9) Gal. 6. 14. (10) Ver. 15. (11) Heb. 2. 11. (12) 2 Pet. 1. 4.

Christ in the *saints,* and the *Father* in Christ, that they might be made perfect in one.[1]

ARTICLE X.

Concerning the universal love and grace of God to all.

God so loved the world, that he gave his only begotten Son, that whosoever believeth in him should not perish, but have everlasting life.[2] And in this was manifested the love of God towards us, because that God sent his only begotten Son, that we might live through him.[3] *So that* if any man sin, we have an advocate with the Father, Jesus Christ the righteous ; and he is the propitiation for our sins ; and not for ours only, but also for the sins of the whole world.[4] *For* by the grace of God he *hath tasted* death for every man.[5] *And* gave himself a ransom for all, to be testified in due time.[6] *Willing* all men to be saved, and to come to the knowledge of the truth.[7] Not willing that any should perish, but that all should come to repentance.[8] For God sent not his Son into the world to condemn the world, but that the world through him might be saved.[9] *And Christ came a* light into the world, that whosoever believeth in *him,* should not abide in darkness.[10] Therefore, as by the offence of one, judgment came upon all men to condemnation ; even so by the righteousness of one, the free gift came upon all men to justification of life.[11]

ARTICLE XI.

Concerning the light that enlighteneth every man.

The gospel was preached to every creature under heaven.[12] *Which gospel* is the power of God unto salvation,

---

(1) John 17. 21, 22, 23.   (2) John 3. 16.   (3) 1 John 4. 9.
(4) 1 John 2. 1, 2.   (5) Heb. 2. 9.   (6) 1 Tim. 2. 6.   (7) 1 Tim. 2. 4.   (8) 2 Pet. 3. 9.   (9) John 3. 17.   (10) Ch. 12. 46.
(11) Rom. 5. 18.   (12) Col. 1. 23.

to them that believe.[1] *And* if *it* be hid, it is hid to them
which are lost, in whom the god of this world hath blinded the minds of them which believe not, lest the light of
the glorious gospel of Christ should shine unto them.[2] And
this is the condemnation, that light is come into the world,
and men *love* darkness rather than light, because their
deeds *are* evil.[3] *And this* was the true light, which lighteth every man that cometh into the world.[4] *By which*
all things that are reprovable, are made manifest; for
whatsoever maketh manifest is light.[5] Every one that
doth evil, hateth the light, neither cometh to the light, lest
his deeds should be reproved : but he that doeth truth,
cometh to the light, that his deeds may be made manifest,
that they are wrought in God.[6] *And they that* walk in
the light, as he is in the light, have fellowship one with
another, and the blood of Jesus Christ his Son, cleanseth *them* from all sin.[7] *Therefore ought we to* believe in
the light, while *we* have the light, that *we* may be the children of the light.[8] *Therefore* to-day, if *we* will hear his
voice, *let us* not harden *our* hearts.[9] *For Christ wept over*
Jerusalem, saying, If thou hadst known, even thou, at least
in this thy day, the things which belong unto thy peace,
but now they are hid from thine eyes.[10] *And he* would
often have gathered *her* children, as a hen gathereth her
chickens; *but they* would not.[11] *For the* stiff-necked and
uncircumcised in heart and ears, do always resist the Holy
Ghost.[12] And are of those that rebel against the light.[13]
Therefore God's Spirit will not always strive with man.[14]
For the wrath of God is revealed from heaven against all
ungodliness and unrighteousness of men, who hold the
truth in unrighteousness.[15] Because what is to be known
of God is manifest in them; for God hath shewed it unto
them.[16] *And a* manifestation of the Spirit is given to every
man to profit withal.[17] For the grace of God that brings
salvation, hath appeared to all men, teaching us, that denying ungodliness and worldly lusts, we should live soberly,

---

(1) Rom. 1. 16.   (2) 2 Cor. 4. 3, 4.   (3) John 3. 19.   (4) Ch.
1. 9.   (5) Eph. 5. 11.   (6) John 3. 20.   (7) 1 John 1. 7.
(8) John 12. 36.   (9) Heb. 4. 7,   (10) Luke 19. 42.   (11) Mat.
23. 37.   (12) Acts 7. 51.   (13) Job 24. 13.   (14) Gen. 6. 3.
(15) Rom. 1. 18.   (16) Ver. 19.   (17) 1 Cor. 12. 17.

righteously and godly in this present world.[1] *And this word of his grace, is able to build up, and give an inheritance among all those that are sanctified.*[2] For the word of God is quick and powerful, and sharper than any two-edged sword, piercing even to the dividing asunder of the soul and spirit, and of the joints and marrow, and is a discerner of the thoughts and intents of the heart.[3] *This is that* more sure word of prophecy, whereunto *we* do well that *we* take heed, as unto a light that shineth in a dark place, until the day dawn, and the day-star arise in the heart.[4] *And this* is the word of faith which *the apostles preached*, which is nigh in the mouth, and in the heart.[5] For God, who commanded the light to shine out of darkness, hath shined in our hearts, to give the light of the knowledge of the glory of God in the face of Jesus Christ.[6] But we have this treasure in earthen vessels, that the excellency of the power may be of God and not of us;[7] for the kingdom of God cometh not by observation, but is within us.

ARTICLE XII.

Concerning Faith and Justification.

Faith is the substance of things hoped for, and the evidence of things not seen.[8] Without *which* it is impossible to please God.[9] *Therefore we are justified by* faith, which worketh by love.[10] For faith without works *being* dead, *is* by works made perfect.[11] By the deeds of the law there shall no flesh be justified.[12] *Nor yet* by the works of righteousness which we have done; but according to his mercy *we* are saved, by the washing of regeneration, and renewing of the Holy Ghost.[13] *For we* are *both* washed, sanctified and justified in the name of the Lord Jesus, and by the Spirit of our God.[14]

----

(1) Tit. 2. 11, 12.　　(2) Acts 20. 32.　　(3) Heb. 4. 12.　　(4) 2 Pet. 1. 19.　　(5) Rom. 10. 8.　　(6) 2 Cor. 4. 6.　　(7) Ver. 7. (8) Heb. 11. 1.　　(9) Ver. 6.　　(10) Gal. 5. 6.　　(11) James 2. 22, 26.　　(12) Rom. 3. 20.　　(13) Tit. 3. 5.　　(14) 1 Cor. 6. 11.

ARTICLE XIII.

Concerning Good Works.

If *we* live after the flesh, *we* shall die; but if *we*, through the Spirit, do mortify the deeds of the body, *we* shall live.[1] *For* they which *believe* in God must be careful to maintain good works.[2] For *God* will render to every man according to his deeds.[3] *According to* his righteous judgment, to them who by patient continuance in well-doing, seek for glory, honour and immortality, eternal life: *For such are* counted worthy of the kingdom of God.[4] And cast not away their confidence, which hath great recompence of reward.[5] Blessed *then* are they that do his commandments, that they may have right to the tree of life, and may enter in through the gates into the city.[6]

ARTICLE XIV.

Concerning Perfection.

Sin shall not have dominion over *such as* are not under the law, but under grace.[7] *For* there is no condemnation to those that are in Christ Jesus, who walk not after the flesh, but after the Spirit; for the law of the Spirit of life *maketh* free from the law of sin and death.[8] *For such are* become dead unto sin, and alive unto righteousness; and being made free from sin, *are become* servants of righteousness.[9] Therefore *ought we* to be perfect, as *our* heavenly Father is perfect.[10] *For* the yoke of *Christ* is easy, and *his* burthen is light.[11] And his commandments are not grievous.[12] *And whosoever* will enter into life *must* keep the commandments.[13] Hereby do we know that we know God, if we keep his commandments.[14] He that saith, I know him, and keepeth not his commandments, is a liar, and the truth is not in him.[15] Whoso-

(1) Rom. 8. 13.   (2) Tit. 3. 8.   (3) Rom. 2. 6.   (4) 2 Thes. 1. 5.   (5) Heb. 10. 35.   (6) Rev. 22. 14.   (7) Rom. 6. 14. (8) Ch. 8. 1, 2.   (9) Ch. 2. 18.   (10) Mat. 5. 48.   (11) Ch. 11. 30.   (12) 1 John 5. 3.   (13) Mat. 19. 17.   (14) 1 John 2. 3.   (15) Ver. 4.

ever abideth in him, sinneth not; whosoever sinneth, hath not seen him, neither known him.[1] Let no man deceive *us;* he that doth righteousness is righteous, even as he is righteous; he that committeth sin is of the devil; whosoever is born of God doth not commit sin; for his seed remaineth in him and he cannot sin, because he is born of God.[2] For not every one that saith Lord, Lord, shall enter into the kingdom of heaven; but he that doth the will of *the* Father, which is in heaven.[3] Circumcision is nothing, and uncircumcision is nothing, but the keeping the commandments of God.[4]

ARTICLE XV.

Concerning Perseverance and falling from Grace.

We ought to give diligence to make *our* calling and election sure, which things if we do, *we* shall never fall.[5] *For even* Paul kept under *his* body, and brought it into subjection, lest by any means, when *he* preached to others, *he* himself become a cast-away.[6] *Let us* therefore take heed, lest there be in any of *us* an evil heart of unbelief, in departing from the living God.[7] *Likewise* let us labour to enter into that rest, lest any man fall after the same example of unbelief.[8] For it is impossible for those who were once enlightened, and have tasted of the heavenly gift, and were made partakers of the Holy Ghost, and have tasted of the good word of God, and the powers of the world to come, if they shall fall away, to renew them again unto repentance.[9] *For he* that abideth not in *Christ* is cast forth, and is withered.[10] *Yet such as* overcome, *he* will make as pillars in the temple of *his* God, and they shall go no more out.[11] *And these are* persuaded, that nothing shall be able to separate them from the love of God, which is in Christ Jesus.[12]

---

(1) 1 John 3. 6.   (2) Ver. 7, 8, 9.   (3) Mat. 7. 21.   (4) 1 Cor. 7. 19.   (5) 2 Pet. 1. 10.   (6) 1 Cor. 9. 27.   (7) Heb. 3. 12.   (8) Ch. 4. 11.   (9) Ch. 6. 4, 5, 6.   (10) John 15. 16.   (11) Rev. 3. 12.   (12) Rom. 8. 38.

ARTICLE XVI.

Concerning the Church and ministry.

The Church of God *is* the pillar and ground of truth.[1]
Whereof the *dear* Son of God is the head.[2] From which
all the body by joints and bands, having nourishment ministered and knit together, increaseth with the increase of
God.[3] *Which* church of God *are* they that are sanctified
in Christ Jesus.[4] *Who* when he ascended up on high, gave
gifts unto men : And he gave some apostles, some prophets,
some evangelists, some pastors and teachers, for the perfecting of the saints, for the work of the ministry.[5] *Who
ought* to be blameless, vigilant, sober, of good behaviour,
given to hospitality, apt to teach ; not given to wine, no
strikers, not greedy of filthy lucre, but patient ; not brawl-
ers, nor covetous.[6] Lovers of good men, sober, just, holy,
temperate, holding fast the faithful word, as *they* have been
taught, that *they* may be able by sound doctrine, both to
exhort and to convince gainsayers.[7] *Taking* heed to
themselves and to the flock, over which the Holy Ghost
hath made *them* overseers, to feed the church of God.[8]
Taking the oversight thereof, not by constraint, but willingly ; not for filthy lucre, but of a ready mind ; neither
as being lords over God's heritage, but as being ensamples
to the flock.[9] *And such* elders as rule well, *are* to be
counted worthy of double honour, especially they who labour in the word and doctrine.[10] And to *be esteemed* very
highly in love for their works' sake.[11] As every man hath
received the gift, so *ought* the same to be ministered : if
any man speak, let him speak as the oracles of God ; if any
man minister, let him do it as of the ability which God giveth.[12] *Preaching the gospel*, not with *the* wisdom of words,
lest the cross of Christ should be made of none effect.[13]
Nor yet with enticing words of man's wisdom, but in demonstration of the Spirit and of power ; that *the* faith *may* not
stand in the wisdom of men, but in the power of God.[14]

---

(1) 1 Tim. 3. 15.   (2) Col. 1. 18.   (3) Ch. 2. 19.   (4) 1 Cor. 1. 2.
(5) Eph. 4. 8, 11, 12.   (6) 1 Tim. 3. 2, 3.   (7) Tit. 1. 8, 9.   (8) Acts
20. 28.   (9) 1 Pet. 5. 2, 3.   (10) 1 Tim. 5. 17.   (11) 1 Thes.
5. 12.   (12) 1 Pet. 4. 10, 11.   (13) 1 Cor. 1. 17.   (14) Ch.
2. 4, 5.

Howbeit *such* speak wisdom among them that are perfect; yet not the wisdom of this world, nor of the princes of this world, which cometh to nought; but *they* speak the wisdom of God in a mystery, even the hidden wisdom, which God ordained before the world to *their* glory.[1] Which things they also speak not in the words which man's wisdom teacheth, but which the Holy Ghost teacheth.[2] For it is not *they* that speak, but the *Holy Ghost, or* Spirit of the Father, that speaketh in *them.*[3] Who if *they sow* spiritual things, ought to reap carnal things, *for* so the Lord hath ordained, that they which preach the gospel, should live of the gospel; for the scripture saith, Thou shalt not muzzle the mouth of the ox that treadeth out the corn; and the labourer is worthy of his reward.[4] Yet a necessity is laid upon *them ;* yea, woe is unto *them* if *they* preach not the gospel; and their reward *is,* that when they preach the gospel, they make the gospel of Christ without charge.[5] Not *coveting* any man's silver or gold, or apparel; *but their* hands minister to their necessities, that so labouring, *they may* support the weak; *remembering* the words of the Lord Jesus, how he said, It is more blessed to give, than to receive.[6] *For they are not of the* greedy dogs that can never have enough.[7] *Nor of the* shepherds that look to their own way, every one for his gain from his quarter.[8] That feed themselves, and not the flock.[9] That make the people err, *biting* with their teeth, and *crying* peace, and *preparing* war against all such as put not into their mouths, *teaching* for hire, and *divining* for money.[10] *Nor yet of those which* teach things which they ought not, for filthy lucre's sake.[11] That run greedily after the error of *Balaam* for reward, loving the wages of unrighteousness.[12] And through covetousness, with feigned words, *making* merchandise of souls.[13] Men of corrupt minds, destitute of the truth, supposing that gain is godliness.[14] *But they know that* godliness with contentment is great gain.[15] And having food and raiment, *they are* therewith content.[16]

---

(1) 1 Cor. 2. 6, 7.   (2) Ver. 13.   (3) Mat. 10. 20.   (4) 1 Cor. 9. 11, 14, 9.   (5) Ver. 16, 17, 18.   (6) Acts 20, 33, 34.   (7) Isa. 56. 11.   (8) Ibid.   (9) Ezek. 34. 8.   (10) Micah 3. 5, 11.   (11) Tit. 1. 11.   (12) 2 Pet. 2. 15,   (13) Ver. 3.   (14) 1 Tim. 6. 5.   (15) Ver. 6.   (16) Ver. 8.

ARTICLE XVII.

Concerning Worship.

The hour cometh, and now is, when the true worshippers shall worship the Father in Spirit and in truth; for the Father seeketh such to worship him.[1] God is a Spirit, and they which worship him, must worship him in Spirit and in truth.[2] For the Lord is nigh to all them that call upon him, to all that call upon him in truth.[3] *He* is far from the wicked; but *he* heareth the prayers of the righteous.[4] And this is the confidence that we have in him, That if we ask any thing according to his will, he heareth us.[5] What is it then? *We must* pray with the Spirit, and with the understanding also.[6] Likewise the Spirit also helpeth our infirmities; for we know not what we should pray for as we ought; but the Spirit itself maketh intercession for us, with groanings which cannot be uttered: And he that searcheth the heart, knoweth what is the mind of the Spirit, because he maketh intercession for the saints, according to the will of God.[7]

ARTICLE XVIII.

Concerning Baptism.

As *there* is one Lord, one faith, so there is one baptism.[8] *Which* doth also now save us, not the putting away of the filth of the flesh, but the answer of a good conscience towards God, by the resurrection of Jesus Christ.[9] For John indeed baptised with water, but *Christ* with the Holy Ghost and with fire.[10] Therefore as many as *are* baptised into Jesus Christ, *are* baptised into his death, and *are* buried with him by baptism into death, that like as Christ was raised up from the dead by the glory of the Father, even so they also should walk in newness of life.[11] Having put on Christ.[12]

---

(1) John 4. 23.   (2) Ver. 24.   (3) Psalm 145. 18.   (4) Prov. 15. 29.   (5) 1 John 5. 14.   (6) 1 Cor. 14. 15.   (7) Rom. 8. 26. 27.   (8) Eph. 4. 5.   (9) 1 Pet. 3. 21, 22.   (10) Mat. 3. 11. (11) Rom. 6. 3, 4.   (12) Gal. 3. 27.

ARTICLE XIX.

Concerning eating of bread and wine, washing of one another's feet, abstaining from things strangled, and from blood, and anointing of the sick with oil.

The Lord Jesus the same night in which he was betray-ed, took bread; and when he had given thanks, he brake it, and said, Take, eat, this is my body which is broken for you; this do in remembrance of me: After the same manner also he took the cup, when he had supped, saying, This cup is the new testament in my blood; this do ye, as oft as ye drink it, in remembrance of me; for as oft as ye do eat this bread, and drink this cup, ye do shew forth the Lord's death till he come.[1] Jesus knowing that the Father had given all things into his hands, and that he was come from God, and went to God, he riseth from supper, and laid aside his garments, and took a towel, and girded himself; after that he poured water into a bason, and began to wash the disciples' feet, and to wipe them with the towel wherewith he was girded: So after he had washed their feet, and had taken his garments, and was set down again, he said unto them, Know ye what I have done unto you? Ye call me Master and Lord, and ye say well; for so I am; if then I, your Lord and Master, have washed your feet, ye also ought to wash one another's feet; for I have given you an example, that ye should do as I have done unto you.[2] For it seemed good to the Holy Ghost and to us, to lay upon you no greater burthen than these necessary things. That ye abstain from meats offered to idols, from blood, and from things strangled, and from fornication; from which if ye keep yourselves ye do well.[3] Is any man sick among you, let him call for the elders of the church, and let them pray over him anointing him with oil.[4]

(1) 1 Cor. 11. 23, 24, 25, 26.   (2) John 13. 2, 3, 4, 5. 12 to 15.
(3) Acts 15. 28, 29.   (4) James 5. 14.

8 *

ARTICLE XX.

Concerning the liberty of such Christians as are come to know the substance, as to the using or not using of these rites, and of the observation of days.

The kingdom of God is not meat and drink, but right-eousness and peace, and joy in the Holy Ghost.[1] Let no man therefore judge us in meat or drink, or in respect of an holy day, or of the new moon, or of the sabbath days.[2] *For* if *we* be dead with Christ from the rudiments of the world, why, as though living in the world, are *we* subject to ordinances? *Let us* not touch, or taste, or handle, which all are to perish with the using, after the command-ments and doctrines of men.[3] For now, after we have known God, or rather are known of *him, why should we* turn again unto the weak and beggarly elements, *or* desire again to be in bondage *to* observe days and months, and times and years, lest labour have been bestowed on us in vain.[4] *If* one man esteem a day above another, another esteems every day alike; let every man be fully persuaded in his own mind: He that regardeth a day, regardeth it unto the Lord: and he that regardeth not the day, to the Lord he doth not regard it.[5]

ARTICLE XXI.

Concerning Swearing, Fighting, and Persecution.

It hath been said by them of old, Thou shalt not for-swear thyself, but shalt perform unto the Lord thine oaths: but *Christ* says unto *us,* Swear not at all; neither by heaven, for it is God's throne; nor by the earth, for it is his footstool; neither by *Jerusalem,* for it is the city of the great King; neither shalt thou swear by thy head, because thou canst not make one hair white or black; but let your communication be yea, yea; nay, nay; for what-soever is more than these, cometh of evil.[6] *And* James *chargeth us,* Above all things not to swear; neither by

---

(1) Rom. 14. 17.   (2) Col. 2. 16.   (3) Ver. 20 to 22.   (4) Gal. 4. 9 to 11.   (5) Rom. 14. 5, 6.   (6) Mat. 5. 33 to 37.

heaven, neither by the earth, neither by any other oath ; but let your yea, be yea, and your nay, nay, lest ye fall into condemnation.[1] Though we walk in the flesh, we are not to war after the flesh ; for the weapons of our warfare are not *to be* carnal, but mighty through God to the pulling down of strong holds, casting down imaginations, and every high thing that exalts itself against the knowledge of God, and bringing into captivity every thought to the obedience of Christ.[2] *For wars and fightings come of the lusts, that war in the members.*[3] *Therefore Christ commands,* not to resist evil ; but whosoever will smite thee on the right cheek, to turn the other also.[4] *Because Christians are lambs among wolves.*[5] *Therefore are they* hated of all men for *Christ's* sake.[6] *And* all that will live godly in Christ Jesus, must suffer persecution.[7] *Such* are blessed, for theirs is the kingdom of heaven.[8] *For though they* have lost their lives, *yet* shall *they* save them.[9] *And because* they have confessed *Christ* before men, he will also confess them before the angels of God. *We ought* not *then* to fear them which kill the body, but are not able to kill the soul ; but rather fear him which is able to destroy both soul and body in hell.

ARTICLE XXII.

Concerning Magistracy.

Let every soul be subject to the higher powers ; for there is no power but of God ; the powers that be, are ordained of God. Whosoever therefore resists the power, resists the ordinance of God ; and they that resist, shall receive to themselves damnation : for rulers are not a terror to good works, but to the evil. Wilt thou then not be afraid of the power ? Do that which is good, and thou shalt have praise of the same ; for he is the minister of God to thee for good : but if thou do that which is evil, be afraid ; for he beareth

(1) James 5. 12. (2) 2 Cor. 10. 3, 4, 5. (3) James 4. 1, 2. (4) Mat. 5. 39. (5) Luke 10. 3. · (6) Mat. 10. 22. (7) 2 Tim. 3. 12. (8) Mat. 5. 10. (9) Ch. 16. 25. (10) Luke 12. 8, 9. (11) Mat. 10. 28.

not the sword in vain : For he is the minister of God, a revenger to execute wrath upon him that doth evil). Wherefore we must needs be subject, not only for wrath, but also for conscience-sake : for, for this cause pay we also tribute ; for they are God's ministers, attending continually upon this very thing : Render therefore to all their dues ; tribute to whom tribute is due, custom to whom custom, fear to whom fear, honour to whom honour.[1] *Therefore are we to* submit *ourselves* to every ordinance of man for the Lord's sake ; whether it be to the king, as supreme ; or unto governors, as unto them that are sent by him for the punishment of evil-doers, and for the praise of them that do well. For so is the will of God, that with well-doing, *we* may put to silence the ignorance of foolish men.[2] Yet it is right in the sight of God, to hearken unto *him* more than unto *them*.[3] *And though they* straitly command *us* not to teach in *Christ's* name, *we ought* to obey God rather than men.[4]

ARTICLE XXIII.

Concerning the Resurrection.

There shall be a resurrection of the dead, both of the just and unjust.[5] They that have done good, unto the resurrection of life ; and they that have done evil unto the resurrection of damnation.[6] Flesh and blood cannot inherit the kingdom of God ; neither doth corruption inherit incorruption.[7] *Nor* is that body sown that shall be ; but God giveth it a body as it hath pleaseth him, and to every seed his own body : It is sown in corruption, it is raised in incorruption : it is sown in dishonour, it is raised in glory : it is sown in weakness, it is raised in power : it is sown a natural body, it is raised a spiritual body.[8]

----

(1) Rom. 13. 1 to 7.   (2) 1 Pet. 2. 13 to 15.   (3) Acts 4. 19.
(4) Ch. 5. 28, 29.   (5) Ch. 24. 15.   (6) John 5. 29.   (7) 1 Cor.
15. 50.   (8) 1 Cor. 15. 37, 38, 42 to 44.

CHAPTER XVII.

A short Expostulation, with an appeal to all other professors.

Come, let us reason with you, all ye professors of *Christianity,* of what sort or kind soever ; and bring forth your *Catechisms* and *Confessions of Faith,* to that which by most of yourselves is accounted the touch-stone or rule: And suffer yourselves no more to be blinded, and to err through your ignorance of the scriptures, and of the power of God ; but freely acknowledge and confess to that glorious gospel and light, which the scriptures so clearly witness to, and your experience must needs answer ; as also to these other doctrines, which consequently depend upon the belief of that noble and truly catholic principle, wherein the love of God is so mercifully exhibited to all men, and his justice and mercy do like twins so harmoniously concord ; his mercy in the oft tendering of his love, through the strivings and wrestlings of his light, during the day of every man's visitation ; and his justice, both in the destroying and cutting away of the wicked nature and spirit, in those that suffer themselves to be redeemed through his judgments ; and in the utter overthrow of such, who rebelling against the light, and doing despite to the Spirit of grace, hate to be reformed. Now not only this fundamental principle is clearly held forth in this treatise, but all those that depend upon it, as the real and inward justification of the saints, through the power and life of Jesus revealed in them, their full and perfect redemption from the body of death and sin, as they grow up by the workings and prevalency of his grace. And yet, lest security should enter, there is great need of watchfulness, in that they may even depart after they have really witnessed a good condition, and make shipwreck of the faith, and of a good conscience, with all the parts of the doctrine of Christ, as they lie linked together like a golden chain, which doth very much evidence the certainty and virtue of truth above all heresies, error and

deceit, however so cunningly gilded with the specious
pretences thereof. For truth is entire in all its parts, and
consonant to itself, without the least jar, having a wonderful coherence, and a notable harmony, answering together like the strings of a well-tuned instrument; whereas the principles of all other professors, though in some
things most of them come near, and divers acknowledge
that which is truth; yet in most things they stray from it,
so that their principles greatly contradict and jar one
against another; and though they may allege scripture
for some of their principles, yet they are put strangely
to wrest it, and to deny it for others.   My *appeal* then to,
and *expostulation* with, all sorts of professors, is not to
prove some one or two points by the scriptures, for there
be some general notions of truth, which most, if not all,
agree to—but the whole body of our principles, as they
stand in relation to each other, which none of them all is
able to do.   For, among the many professors, their *Catechisms* and *Confessions of Faith*, I find none, save the
dispensation of truth, now again revealed, but such as in
most of their substantial principles differ greatly, and in
many contradict grossly the plain text and tenor of the
scripture.   I confess there be certain men in this age,
who with some plausible appearance of reality, undertake
this task: These are they that join with, and own not
wholly any imbodied people; but while they pretend a
general love to all, yet find fault with some part of every
sort; while in the mean time they scarce can give any
account of their own religion, and most of them prove at
bottom to have none at all.   These men, I say, may per-
haps acknowledge some general truths, and also hold to
the letter of the scripture in some other things, so as thereby to take occasion largely to judge others, while themselves offer not to bring these good things to practice,
they blame others for the want or neglect of: but such
an enterprise from these men, will not, when weighed,
prove a fulfilling of this matter; seeing it is not enough
to acknowledge many truths, but also to deny and witness against all error; and likewise, not to fall short of
any truth which ought to be acknowledged.   Whereas
these sort of men for the most part, cannot give account

of their faith in many things needful to be believed; and
whatever things they may acknowledge to be true, they
err most grievously, and contradict a truth most needful
to be minded and answered, as is proved hereto, in that
they stand not forth to appear for any of these discoveries
they pretend they have, but make a shift to hide their
heads in times of trial, so as not to suffer for, nor with any.
And through these fine pretences above mentioned, through
their scruples of joining with any, they can cunningly shun
the difficulties of persecutions, that attend the particular
sects of *Christians*, and yet by their general charity and
love to all, claim a share in any benefits or advantages that
accrue to one and all : Such then cannot honestly lay claim
to justify their principles and practices from the scriptures.
But I leave these stragglers in religion, and come again to
the divers sects.

To begin with those that are most numerous : I think
I need not say much to the *Papists* in this case; for they
do not so much as pretend to prove all their dogmas by
the scriptures; since it is one of their chief doctrines,
That tradition may authorise doctrines, without any authority of scripture : yea, the council of *Constance* hath
made bold to command things to be believed, *Non obstante
scriptura*, i. e. though the scriptures say the contrary;
and indeed it were their great folly, to pretend to prove
their doctrines by scripture, seeing the adoration of saints
and images, purgatory and prayer for the dead, the prece-
dency of the bishop of *Rome*, the matter of indulgences,
with much more stuff of that kind, hath not the least
shadow of scripture for it.

Among *Protestants*, I know the *Socinians* are great
pretenders to the scriptures, and in words as much exalt
them as any other people; and yet it is strange to see,
how that not only in many things they are not agreeable
to them; but in some of their chief principles quite contrary unto them, as in their denying the divinity of Christ,
which is as expressly mentioned as any thing can be;
And the Word was God, John 1. As also in denying his
being from the beginning, against the very tenor of that
of *John* 1. and divers others, as at large is shewn in the
third chapter of this treatise. Divers other things, as to

them, might be mentioned ; but this may suffice, to stop their boasting in this matter.

The *Arminians* are not more successful in their denying the false doctrine of *absolute reprobation*, and in asserting the *universal extent of Christ's death for all*, than they are short in not placing this salvation in that spiritual light, wherewith man is enlightened by Christ ; but wrongfully ascribing a part of that to the natural will and capacity, which is due alone to the grace and power of God, by which the work is both begun, carried on and accomplished. And herein they, as well as both the *Socinians* and *Pelagians*, though they do well in condemning their errors, yet they miss in setting up another, and not the truth in place thereof ; and in that respect are justly reproved by such scriptures as their adversaries, who otherwise are as far wrong as they, bring against them, in shewing the depravity of man's will by nature, and his incapacity to do any good, but as assisted by the grace of God so to do.

On the other hand, it is strange to observe, how many *Protestants*, the first article of whose *confession of faith*, is to assert the *scripture to be the only rule*, should deny the universal extent of Christ's death, contrary to the express words of scripture, which saith, He tasted death for every man ; or the universality of grace, and a sufficient principle ; which the scriptures assert in as many positive words, as, except we suppose the penmen intended another thing than they spoke, it was possible to do, viz. *A manifestation of the Spirit is given to every man to profit withal : The Grace of God, that bringeth salvation, hath appeared unto all men ;* and many more before mentioned. The like may be said of their denying the perfection of the saints, and asserting the impossibility of any falling away from real beginnings of true and saving grace, contrary to so many express scriptures, as are heretofore adduced in their proper place. But to give all that desire to be undeceived, a more full opportunity to observe how the devil has abused many, pretending to be wise, in making them cloak with a pretence of scripture, false and pernicious doctrines ; I shall take a few of many instances out of the *confession of faith* and *cat-*

echism, made by the divines at *Westminster*, so called; because the same is not only most universally received and believed by the people of Britain and Ireland, but also containeth upon the matter, the faith of the French churches, and of most others, both in the Netherlands, and elsewhere; that it may appear what wild consequences these men have sought, both contrary to the naked import of the words, and to all common sense and reason, to cover some of their erroneous principles.

CHAPTER XVIII.

A short examination of some of the scripture proofs, alleged by the divines at Westminster, to prove divers articles in their Confession of Faith and Catechism.

It is not in the least my design in this chapter, to offer so large an examination of any of their articles, as might be done, nor yet of so many as are very obvious; but only of two or three, to give the reader a taste of them, for example's sake, whereby, as *ex ungue, leonem*, he may judge of most of all the rest, if he will be at the pains narrowly to look over and examine them.

I shall begin with the first chapter, Sect. 1. where they assert two things: First, *That God has committed his will now wholly to writing.* Secondly, *That the former ways of God's revealing his will, as by immediate revelation, are now ceased.* The scriptures they bring to prove it, are first *Prov.* xxii. 19, 20, 21. *Ver.* 19. That thy trust may be in the Lord, I have made known unto thee this day, even to thee. *Ver.* 20, Have not I written to thee excellent things in counsels and knowledge? *Ver.* 21. That I might make thee know the certainty of the words of truth, that thou mightest answer the words of truth to them that send unto thee. *Luke* i. 3, 4. It seemed good to me also, having had perfect understanding of all things from the very first, to write unto thee in order, most excellent Theophilus, that thou mightest

9

know the certainty of those things wherein thou hast been
instructed. *Rom.* xv. 4. For whatsoever things were
written aforetime, were written for our learning, that we,
through patience and comfort of the scriptures, might
have hope. *Mat.* iv. 4. 7. 10. But he answered, and said,
It is written, Man shall not live by bread alone, but by
every word that proceedeth out of the mouth of God.
Ver. 7. Jesus said unto him, It is written again, Thou
shalt not tempt the Lord thy God. *Ver.* 10. Then saith
Jesus unto him, Get thee hence, Satan; For it is written,
Thou shalt worship the Lord thy God, and him only shalt
thou serve. *Isa.* viii. 19, 20. *Ver.* 19. And when they
shall say unto you, Seek unto them that have familiar
spirits, and unto wizards, that peep and that mutter:
Should not a people seek unto their God? For the living
to the dead? *Ver.* 20. To the law and to the testimony,
if they speak not according to this word, it is because
there is no light in them.

But is it not matter of admiration, that men should be
so beside themselves, as to imagine these testimonies do
in the least prove their assertion; or that others that do
not take things merely upon trust, would be so foolish as
to believe them? For, though God made known, and
wrote excellent things to Solomon; though Luke wrote
unto Theophilus, an account of divers transactions of
Christ's outward abode; *For many were never written;*
John xxi. 25. and xx. 30. And there are also many other
things which Jesus did, the which, if they should be written every one, I suppose, that even the world itself could
not contain the books that should be written. And many
other signs truly did Jesus in the presence of his disciples, which are not written in this book. Though Christ
made use of divers scriptures against Satan, and that Isa-
iah directed people to the law, and to the testimony; who
will say *It naturally follows from thence, that God has*
now committed his will wholly to writing? Such a consequence is no more deducible from the scriptures, than
if I should argue thus; *The* divines *of* Westminster *have*
asserted many things without ground, therefore they had
ground for nothing they said. Nay, it follows not by far
so naturally, seeing after the writing of all these passages,

by them cited, according to their own judgment, there were divers scriptures written; so that it had been false for them to assert, *That God had then committed his counsel wholly to writing*, which indeed was not true: So it is most irrational and unwarrantable for any to draw such a strange and strained consequence from their words.

For the second, *That the former ways are now ceased*, they allege, 2 *Tim.* iii. 15. where Paul writes to Timothy, saying, That from a child he (Timothy) hath known the holy scriptures, which were able to make him wise unto salvation through faith, which is in Christ Jesus. And *Heb.* i. 1, 2. God, who, at sundry times, and in divers manners, spake in times past unto the fathers by the prophets, hath in these last days spoken unto us by his Son, whom he hath appointed heir of all things, by whom also he made the worlds. 2 *Pet.* i. 19. We have also a more sure word of prophecy, whereunto ye do well that ye take heed, as unto a light that shineth in a dark place, until the day dawn, and the day-star arise in your hearts.

Which prove the matter as little as the former: If Paul had intended by that to Timothy, what those divines would have, would not they have made the apostles speak a manifest untruth, seeing they themselves acknowledge, that John's revelation was written long after? So that these former ways were not then ceased. As for that of Peter, it is to beg the thing in question, to say *It is intended of the scripture;* and though it were, it proves not the case at all. That of the Hebrews is so far from asserting the matter they would have it, that it may be very aptly brought to prove the quite contrary; for God indeed speaks to us now by his Son: But to infer from thence, *That the Son speaks only to us by the scriptures*, remains yet unproved: And for the apostle to have there asserted it, had been false; seeing the *revelations*, which he and others afterwards had, were inward, and so such were not ceased. And if we may trust the same apostle better than these men, he tells us, That so soon as Christ was revealed in him, he went straight and obeyed. And the same apostle tells us, that Except Christ be in us, we are reprobates; surely he is not dumb in us, seeing he says, He will dwell in us, and walk in us, and be with us to the end of the world. And John tells us, that the inward anointing is to teach us all things; so that we need not, as to any absolute necessity, any man to teach us. How then is this ceased, seeing God speaks to us by Christ, and Christ must be in us? Surely these men have not herein followed the rule of the scriptures; but rather endeavoured most grossly to wrest them, and make of them a nose of wax, notwithstanding their pretences as to the contrary in their sixth section, where they say, *All things necessary are either expressly set down, or by good and necessary consequences may be deduced.* Now that these two former assertions are not expressly set down, they will not deny; whether they follow by sound consequence, any understanding man may judge, by what is above observed.

There are divers other things, in the same chapter, which will not abide the test, for which the scripture proofs, as alleged by them, are most ridiculous; which for brevity's sake I have omitted.

In Chap. 21. Sect. 7. where they say, That *the Sabbath from the resurrection of Christ, was changed into the first day of the week, which in scripture,* say they, *is called the Lord's day, and is to be continued to the end of the world as the* Christian *sabbath.* In which they assert three things.

First, *That the first day of the week is come in place of the seventh for a Sabbath:* To prove which they allege, 1 *Cor.* xvi. 1, 2. Now concerning the collection for the saints, as I have given order to the churches of Galatia, even so do ye: Upon the first day of the week, let every one of you lay by him in store, as God hath prospered him, that there be no gathering when I come. *Acts* xx. 7. And upon the first day of the week, when the disciples came together to break bread, Paul preached to them, ready to depart on the morrow, and continued his speech until midnight.

That these proofs assert not the things expressly, we need not, I suppose, dispute. Now to say, that because Paul desired the Corinthians to lay something by them in store that day; or because he broke bread, and continued his speech until midnight; therefore the first day of the week is come in place of the sabbath, is a consequence more remarkable for its sottishness, than to be credited for its soundness. Indeed to make so solemn an article of faith, as these men would have the morality of the first day of the week to be, would need a more positive and express authority. The text doth clearly enough tell the reason of the disciples meeting so frequently, and of Paul's preaching so long, because he was ready to depart to-morrow; it speaks not a word of its being sabbath.

Their second assertion, *That the first day of the week is therefore called the Lord's day,* is drawn yet more strangely from that of *Rev.* i. 10. I was in the Spirit on the Lord's day, and heard behind me a great voice, as of a trumpet; whereas no particular day of the week is mentioned: So for them to say John *meaned the first day of the week* hath no proof but their own bare assertion.

For their third assertion, *That it is to be continued to the end of the world, as the* Christian *sabbath,* they allege these scriptures, *Exod.* xx. 8, 10, 11. Remember the sabbath-day to keep it holy; but the seventh day is the sabbath of the Lord thy God; in it thou shalt not do any work, thou, nor thy son, nor thy daughter, thy man servant, nor thy maid servant, nor thy cattle, nor the stranger which is within thy gates; for in six days the Lord made heaven and earth, the sea, and all that in them is, and rested the seventh day: wherefore the Lord blessed the sabbath-day and hallowed it. *Isa.* lvi. 2, 4, 6, 7. *Mat.* v. 17, 18. Think not that I am come to destroy the law, or the prophets; I am not come to destroy, but to fulfil; for verily, I say unto you, till heaven and earth pass, one jot or one tittle shall in no wise pass from the law, till all be fulfilled.

If they prove any thing, they must needs prove the continuance of the seventh day, seeing in all the law there is no mention made of the first day of the week being a sabbath. If these may be reckoned good and sound consequences, I know no absurdities so great, no heresies so damnable, no superstitions so ridiculous, but may be cloaked with the authority of the scripture.

In their 27th chapter, and the first, second, and third

9 *

sections, they speak at large of the definition and nature of *Sacraments ;* but in all the scriptures they bring, there is not one word of *sacraments :* The truth is, there was a good reason for this omission; for such a thing is not to be found in all the bible. For them to allege, that the thing signified, is to be found in scripture, though that be also a begging of the question, will not excuse such, who elsewhere aver, *the whole counsel of God is contained in the scripture,* to forsake and reject the tenor thereof, and scrape out of the rubbish of the Romish tradition, for that which is reckoned by themselves so substantial a part of their faith.

In their fourth section they assert two things ; first, *That there are two only sacraments under the gospel.* Secondly, *that these two are baptism and the supper.*

To prove which they allege, *Mat.* xxviii. 19. Go ye therefore and teach all nations, baptizing them in the name of the Father, and of the Son, and of the Holy Ghost. 1 *Cor.* xi. 20. 23. When ye come together therefore into one place, this is not to eat the Lord's supper. For I have received of the Lord, that which also I delivered unto you, that the Lord Jesus the same night in which he was betrayed, took bread. 1 *Cor.* iv. 1. Let a man so account of us, as of the ministers of Christ, and stewards of the mysteries of God. *Heb.* v. 4. And no man taketh this honour to himself, but he that is called of God, as was Aaron.

Now granting there was such a thing as *sacraments,* to be so solemnly performed, all that these scriptures will prove is, That these two were appointed to be performed; but that there are only two, or that these are they, which is the thing asserted and incumbent to be proved, there is not the least shadow of proof alleged ; for, according to their own definition of a sacrament, in the larger catechism, where they say, *The parts of a sacrament are two, the one an outward and sensible sign, used according to Christ's own appointment ; the other, an inward and spiritual grace thereby signified ;* both the *washing of one another's feet,* and the *anointing of the sick with oil,* doth answer to it, and many other things. So that the probation of a *sacrament* at all, or of their being two, seven, yea, or seventy, is all alike easy ; seeing neither name nor number is to be found in the scripture, they being the mere conceits and inventions of men. And yet it is marvellous to see, with how great confidence some men do assert the scripture to be their rule, while they build up so considerable parts of their doctrine, without the least scripture foundation.

Thus I thought fit to pitch upon these three, viz., The *scriptures*, *sabbath*, and *sacraments*, because these be three of the main things for which we the Quakers are chiefly cried out against, and accused, as believing erroneously concerning them. Now what we believe concerning these things, and how agreeable our testimony herein is to the scriptures, is heretofore sufficiently demonstrated : Also how little scripture proof these have for their contrary assertions to us in these things, notwithstanding their great pretences to scripture, will also appear to the unbiassed reader.

THE END.

THE

ANCIENT TESTIMONY

OF THE

PEOPLE CALLED QUAKERS,

REVIVED.

BY THE ORDER AND WITH THE APPROBATION OF THE YEARLY
MEETING, HELD FOR THE PROVINCES OF PENN-
SYLVANIA AND NEW JERSEY, 1772.

———◦———

PHILADELPHIA:
1843.

THE

ANCIENT TESTIMONY

OF THE

PEOPLE CALLED QUAKERS,

REVIVED.

DEAR FRIENDS,

Having lately, by an introduction to our Book of Discipline, given a short hint how our respective meetings for church affairs do consist, and by what authority and example they came at first to be instituted, we think well at this time, for the further information and encouragement of our youth and others whose faces are turned towards Zion, to signify, that by living experience we find, and can with good conscience declare and testify, that the same blessed Holy Spirit which led us to believe and receive the doctrines and principles of truth, as they were declared by Christ and his apostles in the holy scriptures, did and now doth lead us into the like holy order and government to be exercised among us, as it was amongst the primitive Christians, in sanctification and holiness.

For the church of God is a gathering of " them that are sanctified" by the word of truth, " called to be saints,"* who are members of the body, even the true church, whereof Jesus Christ is the head. But before any can come to be true members of that body, they must witness the fiery baptism of the Holy Ghost, to

---

* 1 Cor. 1. 2.

initiate them into this true church; and as they follow
Christ in the regeneration,* they will witness a purity
of living, and be qualified to act and judge for him,
who in dispensing his Holy Spirit, doth in his infinite
wisdom minister unto every member a measure thereof, which operates diversely " for the edifying of the
body, there being some apostles, some teachers, some
pastors,"† some elders, young men, and babes: for all
are not apostles, elders, nor babes;‡ yet all who are
truly gathered are members, and as such, have a sense
and feeling of the life of the body flowing from the
head Jesus Christ. And whilst they remain in that
sense, acting " with all lowliness, meekness, and long-
suffering, forbearing one another in love, endeavouring
to keep the unity of the Spirit in the bond of peace,"§
they will be endued with right judgment, seasoned
with pure charity and perfect love, which is the bond
of our holy communion and church-fellowship.

And as we become thus initiated and qualified, we
shall be enabled to maintain the holy order and
government above mentioned, in perfect unity; and
according to the degree of faithfulness we are found
in, shall more and more see " the holy city New Jerusalem, coming down from God out of heaven, prepared
as a bride adorned for her husband;"‖ and the river
of water of life proceeding out of the throne of God,
and of the Lamb; which city being the true church,
" had a wall great and high,"¶ signifying the excellency of God's power encompassing those that are
within this church; and keeping out all that would
invade or hurt it. " And this wall had twelve founda-
tions, and in them the names of the twelve apostles
of the Lamb;** which denotes, that the doctrines of
the apostles are to be embraced—and those that are
not founded upon them, to be rejected and shut out
of this holy city, which had but one street; and that

---

* Mat. 19. 28.   † Eph. 4. 11.   ‡ 1 Cor. 12. 28.   § Eph. 4. 2, 3.
‖ Rev. 21. 2.   ¶ Ibid ver. 12.   ** Ibid ver. 14.

is the way to the tree of life, where the true members
of the church of Christ are travelling in the unity of
his blessed Spirit; and so they become "of one heart,
and of one soul,"* as the multitude of them that believed in the apostles' days were; in which precious
unity we shall feel the life of righteousness.

And as we come to feel this life, and therein experience the arisings of this glorious day of love and
light, with the increase of this blessed unity, we shall
more and more witness the glory of this spiritual
dispensation, by knowing God's "tabernacle with us,"†
and his dwelling in us, and the peaceable government
of the Lamb among us, mysteriously signified by the
descending of this holy city. And as we abide here,
we shall with *John* see no more sea;‡ that is, we
shall not degenerate into that outrageous and dividing principle, that has at times prevailed in some that
walked amongst us, to manifest they were not of us;
but shall "present our bodies a living sacrifice, holy,
acceptable unto God, which is our reasonable service; and not be conformed to this world, but trans-
formed by the renewing of our mind, proving what is
that good, acceptable, and perfect will of God;" and
then, none among us "will think of himself more
highly than he ought; but will think soberly, according as God hath dealt to every man the measure of
faith."

For having "gifts differing," as said the apostle,
"according to the grace that is given to us; whether
prophecy, we shall prophesy, according to the pro-
portion of faith; or ministry, we shall wait on our
ministry; or he that teacheth, on teaching; or he that
exhorteth, on exhortation; he that giveth, will do it
with simplicity; he that ruleth, with diligence; he that
showeth mercy, with cheerfulness;" our *love* will be
"without dissimulation—abhorring that which is evil,

---

* Acts 4. 32.   † Rev. 21. 3.   ‡ Ibid. ver. 1.
§ Rom. 12. 1, 2, 3.

cleaving to that which is good; kindly affectioned one towards another, with brotherly love—in honour preferring one another; not slothful in business," but providing things honest in the sight of all men; and yet have our minds kept above the surfeiting cares of the world, by being "fervent in spirit, serving the Lord; rejoicing in hope, patient in tribulation, continuing instant in prayer, distributing to the necessity of saints, given to hospitality, blessing them which persecute us, and not cursing."[*]

We shall also "be of the same mind one towards another, affecting not high things, but condescending to men of low estate: not wise in our own conceits; nor recompense to any man evil for evil, or railing for railing; but overcome evil with good; and as much as lieth in us, live peaceably with all men, having the same love; doing nothing through strife or vain glory, but in lowliness of mind, each esteeming the other better than themselves;" the strongest and best gifted, not despising the meanest, nor they envying the strongest; but all in their respective stations and degrees will "walk by the same rule," be of one accord, "and mind the same thing," heartily joining to maintain charity in all its branches, and carry on the affairs of truth in the lamb-like spirit, to the honour of God and comfort one of another in him; and then we shall demonstrate, that we experimentally know there is "one body, and one Spirit; one Lord, one faith, one baptism; one God and Father of all, who is above all, and through all, and in us all."[†]

By all which it is manifest, that our church fellowship stands in the bond of charity and true unity of the Holy Spirit; the fruit whereof, as saith the apostle, "is in all goodness, righteousness and truth, love, joy peace, long-suffering, gentleness, faith, meekness, temperance, against such there is no law; for the law

---

* Rom. 12. 6, 9—14.   ‡ Ibid. ver. 16, 17.   1 Peter 3. 9.   Rom. 12. 18, 21.   Phil. 2. 2, 3.   Ibid. 3. 16.   Eph. 4. 4, 5, 6.

is fulfilled in one word," saith the same apostle, " even this, Thou shalt love thy neighbour as thyself;" which is that perfect charity we speak of, and desire all may come unto, and be preserved in; so that God, " who is love," may take delight in us, and make his abode with us; and then shall we " walk in the Spirit, and not fulfil the lusts of the flesh, for the flesh lusteth against the Spirit, and the Spirit against the flesh."*

" The works of the flesh are manifest," said the apostle *Paul* to the *Galatians*, " which are these: adultery, fornication, uncleanness, lasciviousness, idolatry, witchcraft, hatred, variance, emulations, wrath, strife, seditions, heresies, envyings, murders, drunkenness, revelling, and such like; and they that do such things shall not inherit the kingdom of God." And the same apostle, when he wrote to the churches of Rome, Corinth, Ephesus, and Colosse, testifying against the like evils, and against " foolish talking and jesting," he added, that " no whoremonger, nor unclean person, nor covetous man, who is an idolater, hath any inheritance in the kingdom of Christ and of God; for because of these things cometh the wrath of God upon the children of disobedience. Be not, therefore," said he, " partakers with them; and have no fellowship with the unfruitful works of darkness, but rather reprove them."†

And the same apostle, speaking of some " who were past feeling, had given themselves over to lasciviousness, to work all uncleanness with greediness: But ye," said he to the believers, " have not so learned Christ: If so be, that ye have heard him, and have been taught by him, as the truth is in Jesus; that ye put off concerning the former conversation, the old man which is corrupt, according to the deceitful lusts; and be renewed in the spirit of your mind; and that

---

* Eph. 5. 9.   Gal. 5. 22, 23. also, ver. 14, 16, 17.
† Gal. 5. 19, 20, 21.   Eph. 5. 4, 5, 6, 7, 11.   Col. 3. 5.

ye put on the new man, which after God is created
in righteousness and true holiness; wherefore putting
away lying, speak every man truth with his neighbour; for we are members one of another." And
after he forbad them " to be angry and give place to
the devil," he would have them that " stole, steal no
more;" and that " no corrupt communication should
proceed out of their mouth; but that which is good
to the use of edifying, that it might minister grace to
the hearers; and that all bitterness, and wrath, and
anger, and clamour, and evil speaking, should be put
away, with all malice."*

And the apostle having testified against those " who
were full of envy, murder, debate, deceit, malignity,
whisperers, backbiters, haters of God, despiteful, proud,
boasters, inventors of evil things, disobedient to parents; without understanding, covenant-breakers, without natural affection, implacable, unmerciful, and such
as held the truth in unrighteousness,"† he saith, " Know
ye not that the unrighteous shall not inherit the kingdom of God? Be not deceived; neither fornicators,
nor idolaters, nor adulterers, nor effeminate, nor
abusers of themselves with mankind, nor thieves, nor
covetous, nor drunkards, nor revilers, nor extortioners,
shall inherit the kingdom of God. And such were
some of you; but ye are washed, but ye are sanctified, but ye are justified, in the name of the Lord
Jesus, and by the Spirit of our God."‡ By this we
may clearly understand, that the vilest of people, as
they give way to the power and word of truth, may
be sanctified, and so become members of the church
of Christ; which is great encouragement for all to
submit themselves to the divine holy hand, that leads
them to repentance and amendment of life.

But we may observe, that notwithstanding the
many cautions and repeated advice of the apostles,

* Eph. 4. 19—31.   † Rom. 1. 29, 30, 31. also, ver. 18.
‡ 1 Cor. 6, 9, 10, 11.

yet some in their days, as in our time, who professed the truth, and seemed in measure redeemed out of the evils of this world, fell into these and the like enormities, which the apostles testified against; and some others who were then gathered into the belief of the principles and doctrines of the gospel of Christ, fell from those principles, as some have done in our day. In which cases, such as stood firm in the faith, had power by the Spirit of God, after Christian endeavours to convince and reclaim those backsliders, to exclude them from our spiritual fellowship and communion, as also the privileges they had as fellow-members : which power, we know by good experience, continues with us, in carrying on the discipline of the church in the spirit of meekness.*

Therefore, we say, as our brethren have heretofore concluded, that where any in the church of God, pretending conscience or revelation, shall arise to teach and practise, however insignificant or small in themselves whether principles or practice, yet if they be contrary to such as are already received as true, and confirmed by God's Spirit in the hearts of his saints ; and that the introducing of these things tends to bring reproach upon the truth, as such as are not edifying in themselves, and so stumble the weak ; those who have a true and right discerning, may in and by the power of God authorizing them, and no otherwise, condemn and judge such things ; and their so doing will be obligatory upon all the members that have a true sense, because they will see it to be so, and submit to it.

Whatsoever innovation, difference, or diverse appearance, whether in doctrine or practice, proceedeth not from the pure moving of the Spirit of God, or is not done out of pure tenderness of conscience, but

* 1 Tim. 1. 20,   2 Tim. 2. 17; 3. 8; 4. 10.   3 John 1. 9.   Gal. 2. 4.   1 Cor. 1. 12; 5. 1.

10 *

either from that which being puffed up, affecteth sin-
gularity, and there-through would be observed,
commended, and exalted, or from the malignity of
some humours and natural tempers, which will be
contradicting without cause, and secretly begetting
divisions, animosities and emulations. by which the
unity and unfeigned love of the brethren is lessened
or rent, all things proceeding from this root and spirit,
however little they may be supposed to be of themselves, are to be guarded against, withstood and denied, as hurtful to the true church's peace and hindrance
of the prosperity of truth.

And now we come to take notice of some things,
that others professing christianity deem lawful, which
are not so to us: as swearing and fighting, or going
to war when required by lawful authority. The first
we testify against, because it is contrary to the express
command of our blessed Saviour, who said, " Swear
not at all;"* and the apostle James writing to the
twelve scattered tribes, who according to their law,
were to " swear by the Lord, and perform their oaths
to him," saith: " But above all things, my brethren,
swear not; neither by heaven, neither by the earth,
neither by any other oath; but let your yea be yea,
and your nay, nay, lest you fall into condemnation."†
By this we believe, that all oaths commanded or allowed by the *Mosaical* law, which took their beginning from want of truth and faithfulness, as well as
the oaths of those times, are totally abrogated, and
instead thereof the speaking of truth established.
And we are greatly thankful to God, that our superiors in Great Britain have been pleased to grant
relief and ease to us in that point, and hope it will be
a firm and renewed obligation upon us to keep peaceable, faithful, harmless and honest towards all the
children of men: and then we shall assuredly be pre-

---

* Mat. 5. 34.   † James 5. 12.

served out of those contests, fallacies, strife and per-
fidies, against which oaths were at first introduced as
a remedy, and are still alleged to be a security.

And since we must not "swear at all," we cannot
administer oaths to others; therefore, let all of our
community, who are or may be concerned as magistrates, be tender of God's honour in this matter.

And as for wars and fightings, they are altogether
unlawful to us, because our Lord and Saviour Jesus
Christ, who for the excellency of his government, is
called "the Prince of Peace,"* in his blessed sermon
upon the mount, commanded that we should "love our
enemies."†

And the apostle Paul exhorts, not to "avenge ourselves;" but "if our enemy hunger, we must feed
him; if he thirst, give him drink."‡ But it is evident,
that war teacheth to hate, famish and destroy them.
The same apostle declares, that we war not after the
flesh,§ nor "wrestle against flesh and blood."‖ But
outward war is according to the flesh, and against
flesh and blood, for the shedding of the one, and destroying of the other. The same apostle saith further,
"The weapons of our warfare are not carnal, but
mighty through God;"¶ so are not the weapons of
outward warfare. And the apostle James testifies,
that wars and fightings come from lusts,** and those
lusts war in the members of carnal men: but such as
have crucified the flesh with its affections and lusts,
cannot indulge them by waging war; nor can the servants of Christ fight, because his "kingdom is not of
this world."†† So that when Peter used the sword,
his Lord and Master reproved him, saying, "Put up
again thy sword into his place, for all they that take
the sword, shall perish with the sword."‡‡ We are
not without sorrowful instances, of some that have

---

* Isa. 9. 6.   † Mat. 5. 44.   ‡ Rom. 12. 19, 20.
§ 2 Cor. 10. 3.   ‖ Eph. 6. 12.   ¶ 2 Cor. 10. 4.
** James 4. 1.   †† John 18. 36.   ‡‡ Mat. 26. 52.

been educated in the peaceable principles here asserted; and yet became so far degenerated from it as to use the sword; and they perished by the sword; which is here mentioned only as a warning to those, who by pursuing the vanity of their minds, may happen to stray out of the pure path of peace, and fall into the like inconveniences.

By all which it may appear, that Jesus Christ, the captain of our salvation, calls those that list themselves under his banner, to bear his cross, and abide in humility, patience, simplicity and true charity, and not any ways indulge the least thought of revenge, or "rendering evil for evil, or railing for railing;"* much less endeavour to advance themselves by the fraudulent stratagems of war; but suffer true love to take place of wrath, and forgiveness to overcome injury and revenge; so the lamb will be preserved before the lion, and "the lion" resign to, and "lie down with the lamb."

And although these testimonies of Christ and his apostles are so clear against wars and fightings, yet our elder brethren, and some of us, formerly suffered much because we could not ourselves bear arms, nor send others in our places, nor pay for buying of drums and other military attire; as also, for not observing those days, which were appointed to crave a blessing for success to the arms of the nation where we lived, or to give thanks for the victories acquired by the effusion of much blood.

There are other things, as giving flattering titles, uncovering the head, and cringing to men; calling the days and months by the heathen names, and drinking one to another, drinking healths, riotings, banquetings, and using games, sports, plays, revels, comedies, and such like, which many of the professors of christianity allow, are not at all lawful to us, because they not only waste that time which is but lent us, and should be spent to the honour of God, but also naturally

* Rom. 12. 17.   1 Peter 3. 9.

draw men from God's fear; and we know the testimony of the Spirit of Truth is against them, and the inward convictions of light and grace .in our own hearts, have prevailed upon us to lay them aside.

And some called Christians, about the first coming forth of our friends, encouraged people to go from their worships to gaming, sportings, music, dancing, wrestling, running of races, and the like; counting it not inconsistent with religion so to do; which was so abominable in the sight of God, that he was pleased to raise a holy zeal in our elder brethren against those ungodly practices, and against drinking healths, banquetings and riotous living, which not only provoke people to excess of eating, drinking, laughter, foolish talking, jesting, and such like things, that are sinful, and in no wise becoming the solidity, gravity and sobriety, which men professing christianity ought to be adorned with; but it is obvious, that such as run into those excesses, bring a scorn and slight upon their profession, to the grief of the honest-hearted; and not only so, but they lay themselves open to commit all such vices as the devil may tempt them to.

And our constant testimony has been, and is, against saying *you* to a single person; not only because it is contrary to the true propriety of speech and scripture language; but it gratifies that proud Haman-like spirit, which possesses the heart of such, who would arrogate to themselves the homage and reverence due to God; requiring to be addressed in such language, as they judge more honourable than that which they bestow upon the Almighty.

And because our ancient friends and elders in the truth could not join with that spirit, they suffered deeply for their innocent testimony against it; and yet, upon all occasions, showed the decent respect due to men, and maintained in the wisdom of God, the true honour and obedience due from subjects to their prince, inferiors to superiors, from children to parents, and servants to masters; whereby the mutual relations betwixt those different ranks and degrees of men, have been, and are asserted and endeavoured to be established, after the manner our Saviour and his apostles were pleased to direct.

Now, before we go further, we think proper to give some account of our principles and practices, concerning those mutual relations or ranks of men. And first, of kings, rulers, and magistrates; as it is our belief, that the powers and government we live under are of the Lord,* so we acknowledge, that fidelity and subjection is due to those who are in authority over us, expecting only the benefit of those good laws which are deemed our birthright as English subjects, and not the protection by gun and sword, which others make the terms of their allegiance. And we faithfully own, that magistracy is an ordinance of God, and "those who rule well are worthy of double honour,"† and deserve to be really valued and much esteemed; not by giving them vain appellations or flattering titles, nor by bowing the body, or uncovering the head, nor by feigned words, called compliments; but by obeying their just and lawful commands, wherein the true honour and subjection due to them doth chiefly consist.

And it has been, and is our frequent concern, according to the pure leadings and dictates of God's Holy Spirit, in our nearest approaches to the throne of his grace, to make "supplication, prayer, intercession, and giving of thanks for kings, and all that are in authority."‡ And we have not been wanting in our respective places and stations, to put people in mind, as the apostle exhorted, to be "subjected to principalities and powers, to obey magistrates, and submit to every ordinance of man for the Lord's sake, whether it be to the king as supreme, or unto gover-

---

* Rom. 13. 1.   † Rom. 13. 2.   1 Tim. 5. 17.   ‡ 1 Tim. 2. 1.

nors, as unto them that are sent by him for the punishment of evil-doers, and praise of them that do well;"* for so the magistrates "are ministers of God to us for good, bearing not the sword in vain, being revengers to execute wrath upon him that doeth evil;"* and for this cause pay we tribute also, for they are God's ministers, attending continually on this very thing.

Yet, when laws and statutes were made, requiring certain conformities, which for conscience-sake could not be complied with by our faithful friends, some magistrates, instead of the sword of justice, took up the sword of persecution against them; nevertheless, they did not resist, but patiently suffered the spoiling of their goods, grievous imprisonments, scourging and banishment from their tender families, friends and relations; choosing, as the holy apostles did in the like case, "to obey God rather than men;"‡ for they could not "but speak the things which they had seen and heard;" and for all this cruel usage and sufferings, they paid their taxes and tributes, "rendering to Cæsar the things which were his, and to God the things that were his;"§ for so was "the will of God, that with well doing, they should put to silence the ignorance of foolish men."‖

And here it is necessary to distinguish between the laws or statutes which occasioned those sufferings, and *the law*, which the apostle said, "is good if a man use it lawfully; knowing this, that the law is not made for the righteous man, but for the lawless and disobedient, for the ungodly and for sinners, for unholy and profane, for murderers of fathers, and murderers of mothers, for man-slayers, for whoremongers, for them that defile themselves with mankind, for man-stealers, for liars, for perjured persons, and for any other thing that is contrary to sound doctrine."¶

---

* 1 Peter 2. 13, 14.   † Rom. 13. 4.   ‡ Acts 5. 29. 4. 20.
§ Mat. 22. 21.   ‖ 1 Peter 2. 15.   ¶ 1 Tim. 1. 8, 9, 10.

Dear Friends,

It is evident that it was designed by those statutes, not only to bring all to one form of worship contrived by human invention; but also to establish a ministry and ministers, called and ordained by men, " many of whom judged the life, grace, and Spirit of God no essential part of their ministry, nor any necessary qualification of their ministers, which judgment of theirs being against the law of the Spirit of life, and the divine institution of our Saviour's spiritual worship, must needs be contrary to sound doctrine."*

Nevertheless, to uphold their human ministry, ample provision was made for maintenance of their ministers; and to extort it from such as could not for conscience-sake, own, hear, or receive their ministry. But, when it pleased God to discover to our friends and elders, that " they who worship the Father, must worship him in spirit and in truth,"† and be brought to the true unity thereof, and not into a mere outward conformity, they were soon led to embrace the ancient, holy, living and free ministry; which at the breaking forth of this day and dispensation of the new covenant, was plentifully bestowed upon men and women, who, having received the true knowledge of things spiritual, and being in measure purified and sanctified, were called, moved, and ordained to minister by the inward power and virtue of the word of life, feeling a peculiar unction from the Holy One,‡ to prepare and supply them in the work of this ministry. And " as every one had received the gift, even so they ministered one to another, as good stewards of the manifold grace of God; approving themselves in much patience, in afflictions, in necessity, in distress, in stripes, in imprisonments,"§ &c.; and as they freely received, they freely gave, seeking the salvation of souls, and keeping the " gospel without charge; coveting no

* R. B. 438, 419.   † John 4. 23, 24.   ‡ 1 John 2. 20, 27.
§ 1 Peter 4. 10.   2 Cor. 6. 4, 5.

man's silver, gold, or apparel."* And this pure, free
and living ministry of the word, does in a good degree,
through the great loving kindness of God, continue
amongst us hitherto.

But those ministers ordained by men, are of a contrary disposition; for "they preach for hire, and divine
for money, and look for their gain from their quarter,
and prepare war against such as put not into their
mouths;"† and so they have always done. And because our friends could not in good conscience con-
tribute to support their false ministry, they stirred up
persecution, and turned the magistrate's sword back-
ward, and the laws against the righteous, which was
also contrary to sound doctrine, as well as the true
use and end of good laws, and far from fulfilling the
royal law according to the scripture, which the apostle
James sums up in these words, "Thou shalt love thy
neighbour as thyself:"‡ Therefore, with what justice
could those statutes be put in execution against our
friends for their peaceable meeting to worship God "in
spirit and in truth," since our most holy Saviour and
Bishop of souls declared, that the "Father seeks such
to worship him."§ And for ever blessed and happy
will they be who are found of him, and willingly submit to his requirings, both to believe on him, and worship him in his own spirit, as also conscientiously to
suffer for his name and testimony.‖

So, dear friends, having by the foregoing hints
briefly observed how the material or carnal sword,
invented by men to execute their wrath and revenge
upon their fellow creatures, differs from the sword of
justice, "ordained of God for punishment of evil-doers,
and praise of them that do well;" as also having in
part showed our duty to kings and rulers, we come
now to treat of those relations between children and

---

* 1 Cor. 9. 18. Acts 20. 33.   † Mich. 3. 11. Isa. 56. 11. Mic. 3. 5.
‡ James 2. 8.   § John 4. 23, 24.   ‖ Phil. 1. 29.

11

parents, servants and masters, whose respective duties
to each other are best expressed in the apostle's words,
who said, "Children, obey your parents in the Lord,
for this is right. Honour thy father and mother,
which is the first commandment with promise, that it
may be well with thee, and thou mayest live long on
the earth."*

And ye "fathers, provoke not your children to
wrath, lest they be discouraged; but bring them up
in the nurture and admonition of the Lord."†

"Servants, be obedient to them that are your masters according to the flesh, with fear and trembling,
in singleness of your hearts as unto Christ, not with
eye-service, as men-pleasers, but as the servants of
Christ; doing the will of God from the heart, with
good will, doing service as to the Lord, and not to
men; knowing that whatsoever good thing any man
doeth, the same shall he receive of the Lord, whether
he be bond or free: but he that doeth wrong, shall
receive for the wrong which he hath done; and there
is no respect of persons. Let as many servants as
are under the yoke, count their own masters worthy
of all honour, that the name of God and his doctrine
be not blasphemed. And they that have believing
masters, let them not despise them because they are
brethren; but rather do them service, because they
are faithful and beloved, partakers of the benefit.
Exhort servants to be obedient unto their own masters, and to please them well in all things, not answering again, or gainsaying; not purloining, but showing
all good fidelity; that they may adorn the doctrine
of God our Saviour in all things." And the apostle
Peter bids "servants be subject to their own masters,
with all fear, not only to the good and gentle, but also
to the froward;‡ for this is thank-worthy, if a man for

* Eph. 6. 1, 2, 3.   Col. 3. 20.   † Eph. 6. 4.   Col. 3. 21.
‡ 1 Peter 2. 18.

conscience towards God endure grief, suffering wrong-fully."*

"Masters, give unto your servants that which is just and equal, knowing also that ye have a master in heaven; neither is there respect of persons with him."†

And as the good apostles were moved in their day, by the Lord's Holy Spirit, thus to exhort, so in a measure of the same spirit, our friends and brethren have in this day been concerned to desire, that parents might be exemplary to their children in conversation, and in keeping out of the vain fashions, customs and pride of the world, by adorning themselves modestly, and in plainness, observing the scripture language, wherein is true propriety of speech: and that a godly care and concern should be upon the minds of all parents to watch over their children, with supplication to the Lord, that they be not drawn away from the innocency, simplicity, and plainness of the way of truth; and in a sense thereof to reach the witness in them, that so they might feel in their own spirit a degree of fear and reverence towards God, instructing them to follow his counsel and obey his voice. And as the tribes of Israel were required of God to teach his precepts diligently unto their children, and talk of them when they sat in their houses, and walked by the way, and when they laid down, and when they rose up, so should parents be concerned to acquaint their children how the Lord led them from one degree of faithfulness to another, in a denial of the world's corrupt ways, language, and customs. But if children reject their parents' or guardians' advice, and prove refractory, they are to acquaint the proper meetings therewith, in order to have further advice and assistance for reclaiming such children.‡

---

* Eph. 6. 5—8.   Col. 3. 25.   1 Tim. 6. 1, 2.   Tit. 2. 9, 10.
1 Peter 2. 18, 19.   † Col. 4. 1.   Eph. 6. 9.   ‡ Deut. 6. 7.
Epistle 1694.

And that all parents be watchful over their children, and careful not to suffer them to get into pride and excess, but to keep them to that decent plainness which becomes the people of God; that the sin of the children may not be upon their parents, nor they exposed to ruin by their parents' neglect, or evil example in word or deed.

And our advice is, that all Friends' children have so much learning as to read the holy scriptures and other English books, and to write and cast accounts, so far as to understand some necessary rules in arithmetic; and for that end let the rich help the poor.

And that Friends of all degrees take due care to bring up their children to some useful and necessary employment, that they may not spend their precious time in idleness, which is of evil example, and tends much to their hurt.

And that it is a very evil thing for children to answer their parents crossly or frowardly; but if they think amiss of what is proposed or said, they should answer soberly and dutifully; for parents are to be regarded and obeyed next to God; and if parents become poor or helpless, their children ought, according to their abilities, to relieve and help them.

In the next place, we are to show what our principles are, concerning that holy ordinance of marriage, which may be reduced to these three particulars.

First, we ought not to marry with those who are out of the belief and profession of the blessed " truth as it is in Jesus," or being of another judgment or fellowship, or pretending to the truth, or making profession thereof, walk not in some good degree answerable thereunto.

Secondly, we ought not to marry by the priests, who take upon them to join people in marriage without any command from the law of God, or precedent, or example, from the holy scriptures for so doing.

Thirdly, we ought not to suffer such kind of marriages to pass among us, which as to the degrees of consanguinity or affinity, or which by reason of pre-contract or otherwise, are in themselves unlawful, or from which there may be any just reflection cast upon our way.

As to the first, we say, that if such as make profession with us, and believe in the light, and own the doctrines and principles of truth, concerning the spiritual appearance and manifestation of our Lord and Saviour Jesus Christ, should marry with such as do not so profess and believe, or with such as profess the truth, and walk not in some good degree answerable thereunto, we cannot have unity with such marriages.

But if any should think it strange that we dislike joining in marriage with those that are not of our profession, though some of them may otherwise be of a civil deportment, we can say from the testimony of the Spirit of God in our hearts, that such mixing in marriages is an unequal yoking, and ought not to be suffered amongst us. And if any should think it lawful, yet some know by experience, that it has not been expedient, but very hurtful, and of ill consequences to the parties, as well as a grief to their honest friends and relations, and frequently ends in woe and ruin of themselves and their children.

And we find that the judgment of truth in the patriarchs and prophets was against mixt marriages in their time, because of the dangerous effects which attended them, in drawing God's peculiar people into corrupt language, heathenish customs, gross idolatry, and at length into a total separation from the holy sanctuary, and protection of the Almighty.*

As to the second, concerning the priests assuming authority to marry, our concurrent testimony with all our faithful brethren and elders, is, and has been, against that usurpation which seems to be an invention to get money. And they themselves have confessed,

---

* Gen. 24. 4. 26. 35. 28. 1, 2. Neh. 13. 23.

11 *

that it is no part of the essence of a marriage: but it is most evident to us, that, after the consent of parents or guardians and relations is had, and other due and orderly proceedings are made, according to the rules and discipline of our religious society, the mutual promise and agreement of the parties before witnesses, in our meetings appointed for such solemnities, amounts to an actual marriage; which the law cannot make void, nor the parties themselves dissolve by release, or other mutual agreement.*

Divers instances might be brought, where marriages have been adjudged good in law, though they were not solemnized by priests, for brevity we omit; and shall only mention a cause which our honourable friend and elder brother George Fox, in his journal, p. 249, said was tried in the assizes at Nottingham, in the year 1661.† The case was thus: Some years before, two Friends were married among Friends, and lived together as man and wife about two years; then the man died, leaving his wife with child, and an estate in copy-hold lands: when the woman was delivered, the jury presented the child heir, who was accordingly admitted; afterwards, one that was near of kin to the child's father, brought that suit, thereby intending to deprive the child of the inheritance; and to effect this, he would prove the child illegitimate, alleging the marriage was not according to law. After the counsel on both sides had done pleading, Judge Archer directed the jury to find the child heir, which they did accordingly.

By this we may understand, how far we are justified in the method of consummating our marriages by mutual promises, which are made with much awe and reverence, in the presence and audience of God's people at their religious assemblies. But it is to be understood, that though we are present at such solem-

---

* 6 Mod. 155. 3 Lev. 376.   † See Hale's Life by by Bp. Burnet, p. 73, 74.

nities, yet we marry none, but are witnesses thereunto, as any other spectators may be.

We thus enlarge upon this head, that none may be imposed upon by those who insinuate, that such as are not married by a priest, their children will be deemed illegitimate; for some pretending to be of us, believed those false suggestions, or made use of them to colour their selfish views, and sinister ends, and so far renounced the testimony of truth, as to be married by priests. Therefore let such weak, ignoble spirits, with all those that promote, or are present at any such marriages, be dealt with, and brought to repent of their out-goings, or be censured for the same.

As to the third and last particular, it is our sense and judgment, that none amongst us move or proceed, in order to marry with such as are pre-engaged or contracted to others, before they are duly discharged or released of that pre-engagement, and that no such procedure be made by such as are within the degrees of consanguinity or affinity, being not allowed by us, or prohibited by the laws and usages of England.

We do not in the least suppose, by what we object against marrying by the priest, or others differing from our way, as if their marriages were void; neither do we take upon us to hinder any to marry otherwise, than by tenderly advising such as are like to go contrary to our discipline; and if they reject our advice, we refuse to be witnesses and concurrers with them. And if they go right, and make regular steps in their procedure, to the satisfaction of the meetings whereto they belong, we allow them to consummate their marriages according to the good order and method which our fathers and elders in the truth, did at first establish in the wisdom and power of God.

And it has been a constant rule, since discipline was first set up amongst Friends, that all their marriages should be laid before the men's and women's meetings, who were to take care that such as come

before them were clear from all other persons on that
account; and that no man should speak to a woman,
in order to marriage, before he had the consent of his
own parents or guardians, and then spoken to her
father and mother, and had their consent; and if she
had no parents alive, but guardians or trustees, then
to speak to them and have their consent, and proceed
accordingly. And we find the reason of this was, for
that some formerly did speak neither to father nor
mother, till they had drawn out and entangled the
affections of the daughter, and that brought great
troubles and discontents upon the parent, and amongst
friends. And therefore this was to be inquired into
in the men's and women's meetings, where the marriages were to be spoken of; and so it is, or ought to
be amongst us. And if parents or guardians have
once consented or approved of such addresses, they
ought not to retract the same, without giving such
reasons as in the judgment of the monthly meeting,
whereto they belong, shall be sufficient for so doing.

And where men and women draw out the affections
one of another, and after a while go to others, and then
do the like, this ought to be censured as a scandalous
practice.

And it hath been the early care, and is the decent
practice amongst Friends, not to consummate second
marriages sooner than a year after the death of a
husband or wife. And that before widows are allowed to marry, care should be taken that provision
be made for their children by former husbands, as
occasion may require.

Dear Friends, we do not prescribe these rules, as
thinking a bare superficial compliance with them to
be sufficient, for we know a formal hypocrite may go
far that way, and not discover himself till his turn is
served. Therefore our desires are, that in this im-
portant affair of marriage, a godly care may come
upon all such as may be concerned therein, as it has

been and is upon the faithful, to know their hearts and spirits truly and sincerely given up in chastity and purity of love one towards another, with a free resignation to the will of God, and holy resolutions to serve, obey, and follow him through the various exercises, difficulties and trials which may attend them in a married state; and as they stand in his counsel, they come to know a holy joining in spirit, and the blessing from above to descend upon them in their undertaking; and when they come to enter into the marriage-covenant, they will according to their growth in the blessed truth, be sensible of God's heavenly and spiritual joining; this is the honourable marriage that is sanctified by the Spirit of God, and owned by his people.

And when man and wife are thus " joined together, let no man put them asunder; but let the husband love his wife even as himself, and as Christ loved the church, and not be bitter against her; and let the wife reverence her husband, and submit and be subject unto him as is fit in the Lord."*

Thus far we think proper at present, to collect and lay down our principles and practice, in order to be published, for the help and service of the youth and weak among ourselves, and for the information and satisfaction of others.

Signed in and by order of the said meeting, this 19th day of the 7th mo. 1722, by

SAMUEL PRESTON.

---

* Mat. 19. 6;—Eph. 5. 33, ver. 25;—Col. 3. 19;—Eph. 5. 32.

PRINTED BY JOSEPH RAKESTRAW.

Lightning Source UK Ltd.
Milton Keynes UK
05 October 2009